Data Stewardship Body of Knowledge

(DSBOK)

Dave Wells

Technics Publications
SEDONA, ARIZONA

TECHNICS PUBLICATIONS

115 Linda Vista, Sedona, AZ 86336 USA
https://www.TechnicsPub.com

Edited by Steve Hoberman
Cover design by Lorena Molinari

First Printing 2025

Copyright © 2025 by Dave Wells

ISBN, print ed.   9798898160319
ISBN, Kindle ed.   9798898160326
ISBN, PDF ed.   9798898160333

Contents

Preface

The *Data Stewardship Body of Knowledge (DSBOK)* is written for people with responsibilities for data quality, data definition, data protection, and responsible use of data. That includes individual data stewards who serve in part-time and full-time roles, data governance leaders who build and sustain stewardship programs, and managers who oversee people or processes where stewardship responsibilities are embedded. The DSBOK is also useful as a resource for anyone who needs to understand the scope of stewardship and how to equip stewards to succeed.

Too often, individuals are designated as data stewards without being given the knowledge, tools, and training to be effective. This book seeks to fill that gap. It does not provide detailed training. Instead, it maps out the breadth of knowledge areas that stewards may need to understand. By doing so, it supports both organizations and individuals as they prepare for the work of stewardship. The content emphasizes breadth, not exhaustiveness. No single steward needs to master all of the topics described here, but all will find guidance to help identify the areas of knowledge that are most important for their specific roles and responsibilities.

This is not a "how-to" manual. It is a catalog of knowledge areas that fall within the scope of stewardship. Each topic is presented with three focal points: what the area is about, why it matters to stewardship, and what kinds of knowledge a steward may need to acquire. The purpose is not to teach the details of each subject, but to provide a structured guide that identifies the learning needed to be effective.

Origins of the Book

The idea of a Data Stewardship Body of Knowledge began with **eLearningCurve** and the creation of the **Certified Data Steward (CDS) program** in 2016. At that time, the Body of Knowledge was an outline used to shape training curriculum and certification exams. It was updated in 2020 and again in 2025.

Through these updates, it became clear that while the outline serves its original purpose of guiding curriculum and exam management, an outline alone cannot meet the broader need for guidance in practice. That broader purpose needs more than a list of topics. It requires expansion—descriptions of each knowledge area that explain why it matters and what stewards should understand. This book fulfills that need, extending the Body of Knowledge from outline to a reference that stewards, governance leaders, and organizations can rely on to grow both individual and collective stewardship capabilities.

I want to recognize **eLearningCurve** (elearningcurve.com) and especially the **Certified Data Steward (CDS) program**

(https://ecm.elearningcurve.com/CDS-s/136.htm), which has shaped the origin and evolution of the DSBOK, and continues to advance the profession of data stewardship.

Acknowledgments

I am grateful to my colleagues Olga Maydanchik and Mark Peco. Their depth of knowledge, thoughtful reviews, and constructive feedback led to meaningful improvements in both the DSBOK outline and the expanded knowledge descriptions that form this book. Their contributions strengthened both the accuracy of the content and its practical value for readers.

Closing Note

The DSBOK is intended as a guide and a reference, not as a one-time read. My hope is that it will support the growth of individual stewards, the maturity of stewardship programs, and the advancement of responsible data practices across organizations. Stewardship is a collaborative and evolving discipline, and this book is offered as a companion for that ongoing journey.

Introduction

What the Book Is and Is Not

This is not a "how-to" manual. Instead, it is a catalog of topics that fall within the scope of what data stewards need to know. Each knowledge topic is presented as a description of what the area is about, why it matters to stewardship, and what kinds of knowledge a steward may need to acquire. It is not intended to teach the details of each subject, nor to summarize all that each topic entails. Rather, it serves as a guide to what you may need to learn.

Breadth, Not Exhaustiveness

No single steward will ever know all of the subjects covered here, nor does every steward need to. Stewardship is diverse. Different roles, activities, and tasks are sure to require different sets of knowledge. The purpose of this book is to map the terrain of stewardship knowledge so individuals and organizations can identify what matters most in their context.

How to Use this Book

Each topic in the body of knowledge is designed to stand alone. The book is not written to be read cover-to-cover, but to serve as a reference that you can return to as needed. If you are a data steward facing a task or situation where you do not feel fully prepared, you can scan the DSBOK outline to locate areas where you may need to develop knowledge, and use the descriptions as a guide to find books, articles, classes, and other learning resources. It is reasonable to expect that you will be adding new knowledge throughout your tenure as a data steward, and this body of knowledge may serve as a guidebook for ongoing learning.

If you are a data governance leader or other individual responsible to develop, shape, and mature a stewardship program, you can use the DSBOK to identify the kinds of knowledge most needed by your stewards. It can help you understand what needs to be known and guide planning for the learning and growth of your stewardship team.

Throughout the book, you'll find occasional figures and tables. While related to the subjects in which they appear, they are not direct illustrations of the text. They are intended to visualize related concepts, provide additional perspectives, and stimulate thought about what the knowledge subject area may encompass.

The book also includes a glossary of data management terms. Not all of these terms appear in the body of knowledge, and not all terms in the body of knowledge are repeated in the glossary. The purpose of the glossary is to support stewards who will encounter unfamiliar terminology as they collaborate with data management professionals and data stakeholders. While it does not eliminate the need for further learning, the glossary provides a ready reference for terms that stewards are likely to encounter and need to understand.

Data Stewardship Fundamentals

Data stewardship provides the foundation for how organizations define, manage, and apply accountability to data. It establishes the people, processes, and structures needed to ensure data is accurate, well-defined, and responsibly used. This section introduces the fundamental concepts of stewardship, describes the different types of stewards and how they are organized, highlights staffing approaches, and identifies the challenges and enablers of effective stewardship programs.

1.1 Definitions

Stewardship is the responsibility to manage something of value on behalf of others. In a business context, stewardship implies a duty of care: stewards are entrusted with protecting assets and ensuring that they are managed and used for the benefit of the broader organization and its stakeholders.

Data Stewardship applies the concept of stewardship specifically to data. A data steward takes responsibility to ensure that data is well-defined, of high quality, and used appropriately. The role bridges business and technology by translating policies into data-driven practices and surfacing data issues so they can be effectively addressed.

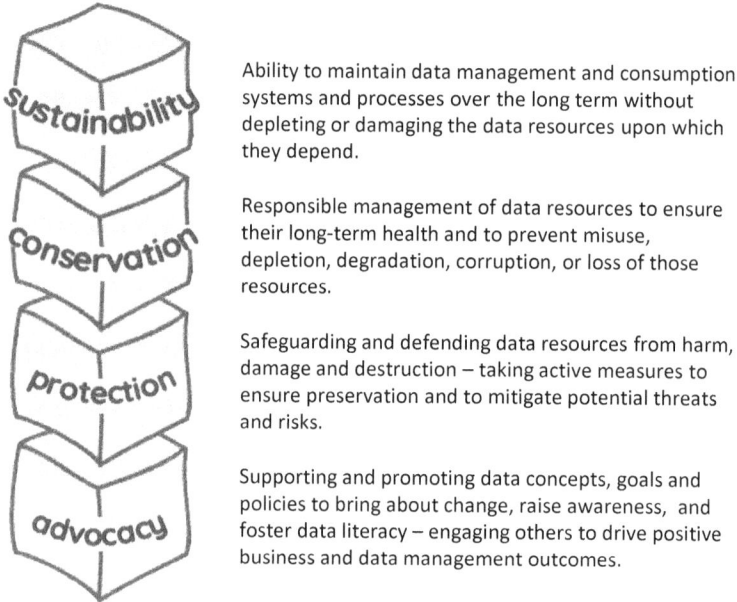

Ability to maintain data management and consumption systems and processes over the long term without depleting or damaging the data resources upon which they depend.

Responsible management of data resources to ensure their long-term health and to prevent misuse, depletion, degradation, corruption, or loss of those resources.

Safeguarding and defending data resources from harm, damage and destruction – taking active measures to ensure preservation and to mitigate potential threats and risks.

Supporting and promoting data concepts, goals and policies to bring about change, raise awareness, and foster data literacy – engaging others to drive positive business and data management outcomes.

Figure 1: Data Stewardship.

The four pillars of data stewardship illustrate complementary responsibilities to ensure that data resources are preserved, responsibly managed, safeguarded, and actively promoted to support long-term business and data management outcomes.

1.2 Data Stewardship Purpose

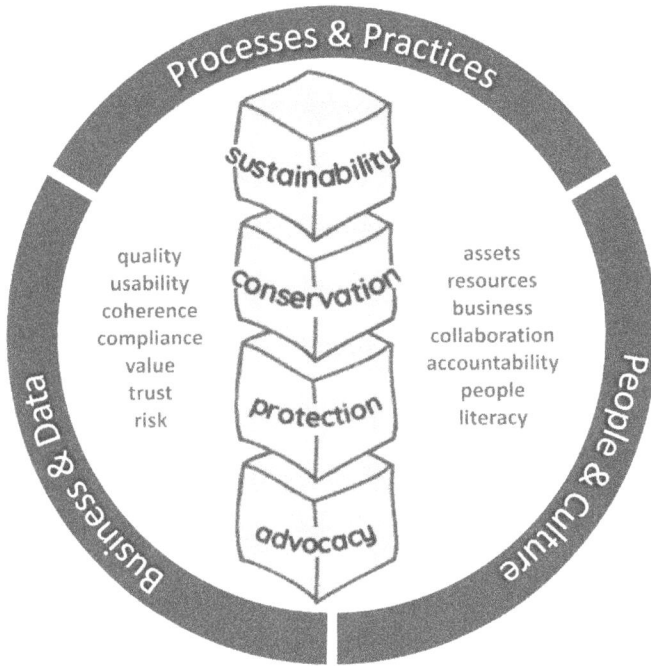

Figure 2: Dimensions of Data Stewardship Purpose.

The purpose of data stewardship extends the four pillars into business, culture, and practices that shape how data is managed and used.

Sustaining and Conserving Data Resources maintains reliable data assets and responsible data management practices. Activities focus on quality, usability, availability, and coherence across domains and systems. Treating data as both an asset and a resource contributes to long-term availability and ongoing business value.

Protecting Data Assets focuses on guarding against the misuse, corruption, and loss of data, as well as preventing intrusion and unauthorized access. Protection efforts defend against data breaches, reinforce compliance with regulatory obligations, build trust with stakeholders, and reduce the risk of operational and reputational harm.

Advocating for Data Value promotes organization-wide recognition of data as a strategic, tactical, and operational asset. Stewards advance literacy, highlight the benefits of standards, and promote recognition of data use cases and value opportunities. Advocacy creates visibility and commitment that turns principles into practice.

Shaping People and Culture influences the environment in which data is managed and used. Data sharing plays a central role, supported by trust, clarity, and literacy that allow data to flow across boundaries. Cultural contributions include fostering collaboration, building shared accountability, and advancing data awareness and data capabilities throughout the organization.

Connecting Business and Data links organizational objectives with data practices and processes to support them. Stewards translate goals into data requirements, interpret the realities of data systems for decision makers, and facilitate dialogue when perspectives differ. This connection brings together diverse viewpoints so that data policies, systems, and practices work in harmony with business goals.

1.3 Data Stewardship Organizations

Kinds of Data Stewards: Organizations often distinguish between different kinds of stewards. Business data stewards focus on the meaning, definition, and use of data within business processes. Technical data stewards are concerned with metadata, lineage, and the systems that store and move data. Domain stewards provide subject-matter expertise in specific areas, such as customer, product, or financial data.

Reporting Relationships: Stewards may report through various organizational lines, depending on the context. Some are embedded in business units, others in IT or data offices, and many operate in hybrid structures. Clear reporting relationships are crucial for accountability and preventing confusion when stewardship responsibilities overlap with operational or technical roles.

		Subject/Object Data Steward (aka Domain Data Steward)	Data for one subject or data entity Work across multiple business processes & systems
Oversight of enterprise-wide data policies / Coordinate efforts of data stewardship team	Enterprise Data Steward	Business Unit Data Steward (aka Business Function Data Steward)	Critical data for one business unit or function Focus on critical data created and used by the unit
		Process Data Steward	Critical data for one business process Manage data flow across multiple business units
		Project/System Data Steward	Data for one or more IT systems or projects Oversight and advising of technical implementations

Figure 3: Kinds of Data Stewards.

The various kinds of data stewards reflect the diverse responsibilities to manage data across domains, functions, processes, and systems.

1.4 Data Stewardship Staffing

Full-Time versus Part-Time: In most organizations, stewardship begins as a part-time responsibility assigned to subject matter experts or business analysts. As programs mature, dedicated full-time stewardship positions are likely to be created for critical data domains. Full-time positions provide continuity and focus that strengthen stewardship effectiveness and increase stewardship visibility across the organization.

Role versus Job Title: The role of Data Steward is often performed without having a formal job title. Many part-time stewards hold business titles such as Financial Analyst, Operations Manager, and other business functional titles. They assume stewardship responsibilities because they work with the data, possess data subject expertise, and have a strong interest in the responsible management of the data. Part-time stewards often hold functional business titles, while full-time stewards are more likely to have the explicit title of Data Steward. A clear title provides recognition and credibility that strengthen stewardship effectiveness.

Who Becomes a Data Steward?

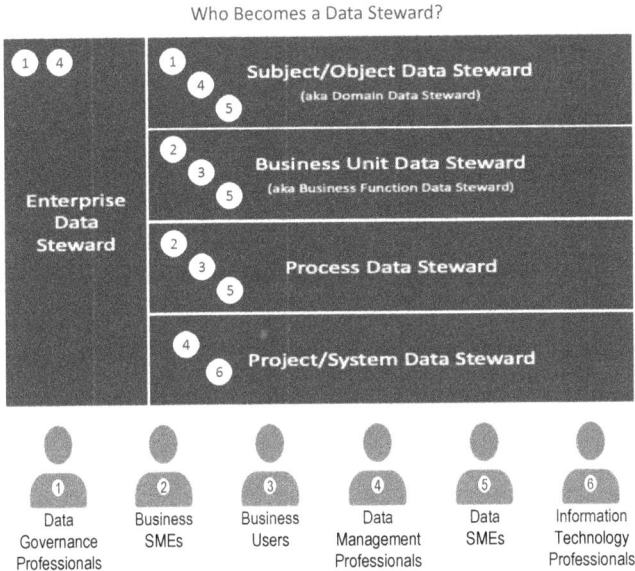

Figure 4: Data Stewardship Staffing.

Data stewards come from diverse backgrounds.
Matching background and experience with steward responsibilities helps to
build strong and collaborative stewardship teams.

Domain Expertise: Stewards must understand the business processes and data domains they represent. Domain expertise enables them to recognize data issues, evaluate quality, and confirm that definitions and policies align with actual business practices.

Capacity and Coverage: A common challenge in stewardship programs is staffing with enough stewards to provide adequate coverage across all critical data domains. Staff must balance capacity with workload so that issue resolution, metadata management, and literacy support are effective and sustainable.

1.5 Organizational Challenges for Data Stewardship

Cross-Functional Friction: Stewardship often requires coordination across multiple departments with differing priorities. Misalignment can cause delays or resistance when defining standards or resolving issues.

Territorialism and Resistance to Data Sharing: Departments may guard their data, viewing stewardship as a threat to autonomy. Overcoming territorialism requires leadership support and a culture that values data as a shared enterprise asset.

Unclear Ownership: Without a clear delineation of decision-making authority and accountability, issues can stall. Ambiguity surrounding who owns specific data domains undermines the effectiveness of stewardship.

Resistance to Governance: Stewardship depends on governance to provide structure and authority. Resistance to governance processes may surface when policies are perceived as constraints rather than enablers.

Overlapping Responsibilities: Data-related responsibilities often overlap among business, IT, compliance, and analytics functions. Stewardship must define boundaries and promote collaboration rather than duplication.

1.6 Data Steward Characteristics

Knowledge and Experience: Effective data stewards bring a balanced blend of knowledge and experience. Their knowledge includes understanding business processes, regulatory requirements, organizational priorities, and the meaning and context of the data they manage. Experience is grounded in the business and technical roles that they have filled, where they gained practical understanding of how data supports decision-making, drives business processes, and shapes outcomes. This combination of formal knowledge and applied experience equips stewards to interpret data in context, anticipate downstream impacts, and participate meaningfully in business and technical conversations.

Skills and Competencies: Stewards need a balanced mix of data knowledge, problem-solving ability, and people skills. They must understand how data is defined, governed, and used across business and technical contexts, and apply that understanding to evaluate issues and guide resolution. Just as critical, they must be able to work effectively with others, applying facilitation and consensus-building skills.

Facilitation and Communication Capabilities: Stewards must be able to bring people together around shared data challenges. This involves guiding discussions, clarifying issues, and helping stakeholders with different priorities reach common ground. Effective stewards listen actively, restate ideas to confirm shared understanding, and reframe problems when needed to open new paths toward resolution. They also educate others by explaining data concepts in plain language, encouraging adoption of standards, and promoting a culture of data literacy. In practice, their ability to foster collaboration and maintain trust often determines whether stewardship efforts succeed or stall.

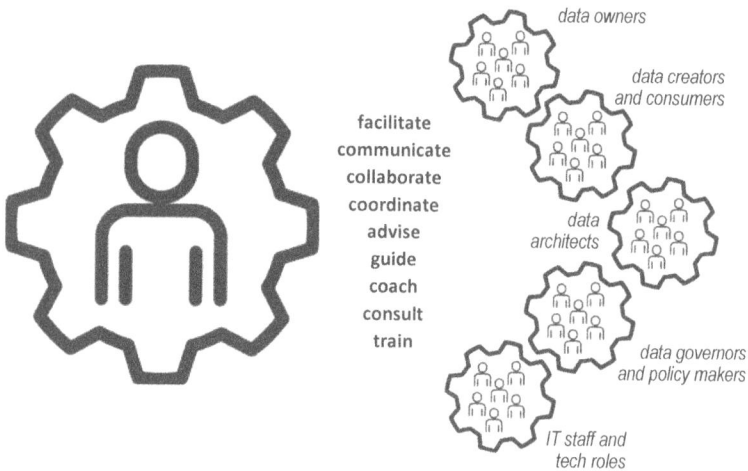

Figure 5: Data Steward as Facilitators and Communicators.

Data stewards use facilitation and communication skills to bring stakeholders together, build shared understanding, and foster collaboration around data.

1.7 Stewardship Metrics and Measures

Issue Resolution: Key metrics include the number of issues logged, average resolution time, and percentage resolved within agreed service levels. These metrics provide visibility into how effectively data issues are being managed. They demonstrate responsiveness to business needs and highlight where data stewardship has an impact.

Data Quality: Stewards monitor data quality through metrics that reflect four dimensions: correctness, integrity, usability, and objectivity. Correctness addresses accuracy, completeness, and timeliness. Integrity covers consistency, valid structures, and reliable relationships. Usability reflects accessibility and clarity for intended users. Objectivity addresses the absence of bias and distortion.

Metadata Coverage: Metadata coverage metrics show the degree of completeness for the definition and documentation of data assets. Coverage of critical data elements (CDEs) is essential, and meaningful measures often extend to other important data domains for a full view of metadata completeness. Metrics examples include the percentage of CDEs with approved business definitions, the proportion of data sets represented in glossaries, and the extent of lineage documentation across systems. These metrics highlight the maturity of metadata management and its role in enabling consistent use of data across the organization.

Compliance: Compliance metrics reflect the degree to which data practices align with established policies, standards, and regulatory requirements. Measures may include adherence to data retention rules, the percentage of data sets that meet classification and protection standards, the successful completion rate of required audits and reviews, and many other ways to quantify how stewardship activities align with regulatory obligations, internal policies, and risk management practices. These metrics demonstrate whether data is being managed responsibly and in accordance with both internal expectations and external obligations.

Engagement: Engagement metrics indicate how actively people participate in stewardship activities and make use of stewardship resources. Examples include attendance at governance forums, the volume of issues logged and resolved through stewardship channels, and the level of adoption for glossaries or standards. These metrics demonstrate the degree to which stewardship is embedded in day-to-day practices and supported across the organization.

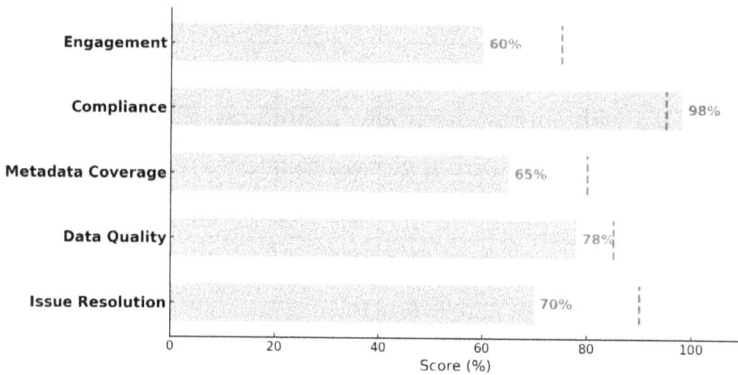

Figure 6: Data Stewardship Metrics – A Dashboard Example.

Use dashboards and scorecards to track stewardship metrics, monitor progress, and know where attention is needed to strengthen data practices.

1.8 Stewardship Tools and Technologies

Data Catalogs and Glossaries: Data catalogs and glossaries are practical tools that are used to make data understandable and usable. Glossaries provide business users with clear definitions and classifications, thereby reducing ambiguity of terms. Catalogs extend this by linking definitions to data assets, helping people discover what data exists, where it resides, and how it can be applied. Stewards and users rely on these tools to locate trusted data, understand its context, and align business meaning with technical implementation.

Data Quality Platforms: Data quality platforms provide profiling, monitoring, and rule execution aligned to key dimensions of quality. They assess correctness through measures of accuracy, completeness, and timeliness. They evaluate integrity by checking consistency, structural soundness, and valid relationships. They support usability by tracking accessibility, clarity, and readiness for use. They also help assess objectivity by detecting patterns that may indicate bias or distortion. These capabilities make data quality visible and measurable in ways that directly support stewardship.

Lineage and Traceability Tools: Lineage and traceability tools document how data moves and changes from point-of-origin to points-of-use. They capture technical transformations such as filtering, aggregations, calculations, and ETL steps, as well as processes that blend data from multiple sources. They also record business context, for example, how a calculated field is derived for reporting purposes, confirming that both the mechanics and meaning of data changes are transparent. By providing visibility into data flows and transformations, lineage tools enable impact analysis when data definitions change, support regulatory requirements for traceability, and build trust in analytical results by showing how they were produced. Traceability also helps identify gaps, redundancies, or risks in data movement, making it a key capability for stewardship in complex environments.

Collaboration and Knowledge Platforms: Collaboration and knowledge platforms provide spaces where stewards and stakeholders share information, coordinate activities, and build a collective understanding of data. They support issue discussions, capture decisions, and make stewardship guidance accessible to a broad audience. These tools also promote data literacy by providing channels for training, best practices, and peer-to-peer support. By making stewardship visible and interactive, they help embed it into everyday work.

Two

Data Steward Skills

Data Stewardship Skills enable stewards to work across boundaries, resolve issues, and support responsible use of data. These skills fall into three groups. People skills emphasize communication, facilitation, collaboration, and coaching. Work management skills include problem-solving, issue resolution, change management, and organizing stewardship activities. Information management skills provide the literacy to understand data management, business processes, and technical environments. Together, these skills equip stewards to bridge perspectives and assure that stewardship delivers value to the organization.

Figure 7: The Stewardship Skillset.

Three kinds of stewardship skills enable stewards to communicate effectively, get things done, and promote good data practices across the organization.

2.1 People Skills

Communication Skills include presenting information in verbal, written, and visual forms. Awareness of the audience is essential, and observing unspoken reactions and feedback is a key skill. Listening is as important as presenting information, and good stewards practice active listening. Strong communication reduces ambiguity, builds trust, and helps to create a shared understanding of data issues.

Facilitation Skills focus on guiding discussions and decision-making. Stewards work to keep conversations productive, surface diverse perspectives, and help participants move toward shared understanding and agreement. Good facilitation assures that stewardship efforts do not stall when priorities conflict or when decisions require alignment across functions.

Collaboration Skills are essential because stewardship work crosses boundaries of business units, functions, and systems. Effective collaboration involves building trust, coordinating activities, and sustaining cooperation when responsibilities overlap. These skills allow stewards to maintain momentum and foster relationships that support long-term stewardship success.

Coaching Skills enable stewards to help others grow in their understanding and use of data. Coaching may involve answering questions, providing guidance on best practices, or supporting the adoption of new policies and standards. By encouraging others and sharing knowledge, stewards strengthen data literacy and embed stewardship into everyday work.

2.2 Work Management Skills

Problem-Solving Skills involve identifying issues, analyzing their causes, and developing practical solutions. Stewards apply structured thinking as a process: starting with visible symptoms, investigating to uncover root causes, and then developing and implementing responses and solutions that address the underlying problems.

Issues Management Skills focus on logging, tracking, and resolving data-related issues. This includes prioritizing problems, coordinating stakeholders, and monitoring progress toward resolution. Effective issues management makes data problems visible, clarifies accountability, and assures that they are resolved in a timely manner.

Change Management Skills are needed because stewardship often involves introducing new policies, standards, and practices. Stewards help people adapt by communicating the reasons for change, addressing their concerns, and guiding the adoption process. These skills reduce resistance and increase the likelihood that changes will be sustained.

Planning and Project Skills involve organizing stewardship activities, initiatives, and teams. This includes planning tasks, setting priorities, and coordinating resources to meet goals. Strong planning and project skills support stewardship efforts that are structured, efficient, and aligned with organizational priorities.

2.3 Information Management Skills

Data Skills give stewards the literacy to understand how data is defined, classified, and managed. This includes familiarity with glossaries, metadata, quality dimensions, and policy requirements such as privacy and retention. Data skills help stewards recognize issues and support best practices in describing, managing, and using data.

Business Skills connect stewardship to the processes and decisions that rely on data. Stewards need to understand the business processes within their scope of responsibility, such as customer service, order fulfillment, and financial reporting, and recognize how data supports them. These skills help stewards keep data practices aligned with business objectives and priorities.

Technical Skills involve awareness of the systems, architectures, and flows that move and store data. Stewards do not require deep technical expertise, but they should have sufficient understanding to converse with technologists, anticipate the impact of changes, and connect business requirements with technical implementations.

THREE

Metadata Management

Metadata Management is a critical element of data management. Metadata is information about how data is defined, captured, managed, processed, and used. Metadata gives context to data by describing its meaning, structure, origins, and use, with the goals of making it discoverable and trustworthy. Just as financial resources cannot be managed without financial data, and human resources cannot be managed without HR data, data resources cannot be managed without metadata. For stewards, familiarity with metadata concepts is essential because stewardship activities depend on the ability to interpret, communicate, and align definitions across business and technical domains.

METADATA COLLECTION	METADATA STORAGE	METADATA ACCESS	METADATA CONSUMPTION
Metadata Creation	Data Catalogs	Data Catalogs	Find & Understand Data
Metadata Discovery	Metadata Repositories	Metadata Connectors	Manage Data Lifecycles
Metadata Acquisition	Tool-Specific Metadata Stores	Metadata APIs	Reporting, Analytics, AI/ML
	File & Database Management Systems		Data Management Automation

METADATA TOOLS & TECHNOLOGY

METADATA INVENTORY

Business Metadata	Technical Metadata	Operational Metadata	Social Metadata

METADATA MANAGEMENT

Metadata Governance	Data Cataloging	Metadata Interoperability	Metadata Consolidation	Metadata Freshness & Quality	Metadata Maintenance & Disposal

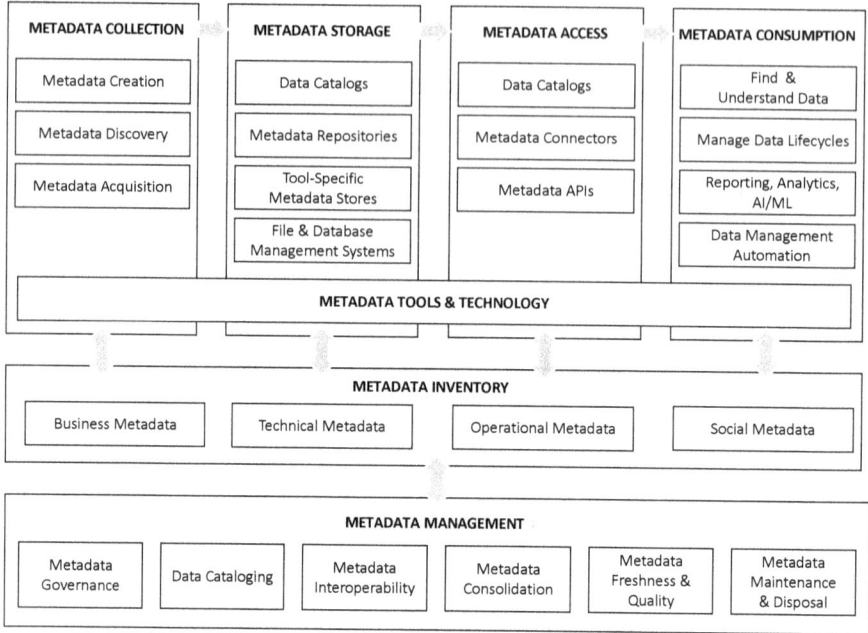

Figure 8: An Architectural View of Metadata Management.

This diagram illustrates the metadata perspectives that stewards need to understand to manage metadata effectively. Key concepts include the types of metadata—business, technical, operational, and social—along with metadata lifecycle, usage, governance, repositories, and technologies.

3.1 Metadata Concepts

Types of Metadata include business, technical, operational, and social. Each type provides a different perspective for how data is described and understood. Business metadata explains meanings, rules, and definitions that make data clear to business users. Technical metadata documents structures, formats, and processing details within systems. Operational metadata records how data moves, changes, and is used in workflows and processes. Social metadata adds user-generated context such as ratings, comments, and usage tags. For stewards, recognizing these types is essential because metadata management depends on aligning business, technical, operational, and social perspectives into a coherent view.

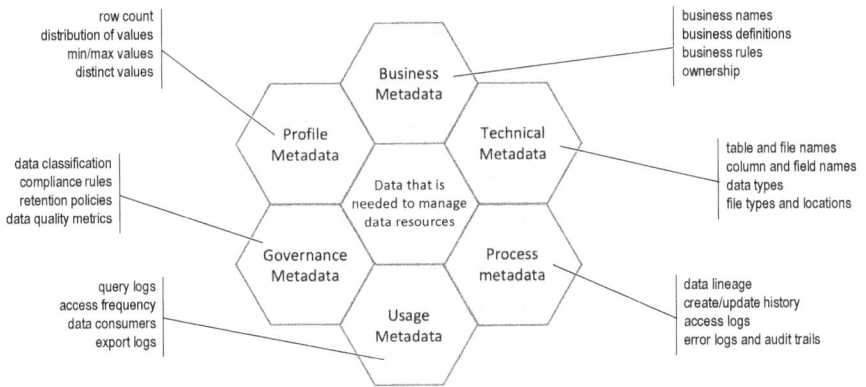

Figure 9: Kinds of Metadata.

Metadata takes many forms, each offering a view of how data is defined, managed, and applied. Together, they create a complete picture that stewards use to align meaning, structure, and use.

Metadata Users and Uses are many and varied. Both people and software use metadata when working with data. Business metadata enables data discovery, understanding, and trust. Stewards use it to achieve alignment between data and business purpose and to support accurate reporting and information services. Technical metadata supports schema management, integration design, and data protection. Stewards collaborate with technical teams to implement data flows that are well understood and documented, and to confirm that protection measures are built into data architecture. Process metadata provides insight into data movement, transformation, and lineage. It is vital for audits, regulatory compliance, troubleshooting, and impact analysis. Stewards use this metadata to trace the origins of data issues and understand changes across data pipelines. Usage metadata captures how data is accessed and consumed. Stewards rely on this metadata to support performance monitoring, detect anomalies, and guide decisions about provisioning, personalization, and resource prioritization. Governance metadata plays a central role in stewardship. It includes classification, policy enforcement, security, and audit trails. Stewards must understand how governance metadata is applied and monitored to ensure data compliance and traceability. Profile metadata informs assessments of data quality, consistency, and value distribution. Stewards use it to evaluate data integrity, monitor transformation results, and identify anomalies that may indicate quality concerns.

	PEOPLE										TOOLS							
	Architects (data and systems)	Auditors	Business and Data Analysts	Compliance and Risk Teams	Data Engineers	Data Governors	Data Scientists	Data Stewards	Database Administrators	System Developers	BI and Analytics	Data Catalogs	Business Glossaries	Data Integration / ETL	Security and Compliance	Data Warehousing	Data Lake / Lakehouse	Data Quality
Business Metadata																		
Technical Metadata																		
Process Metadata																		
Usage Metadata																		
Governance Metadata																		
Profile Metadata																		

Figure 10: Metadata Users.

This table illustrates many of the common users of metadata and their typical metadata needs. Note that all users need to have governance metadata.

Metadata Subjects and Sources identify the objects being described (the subjects) and where metadata originates (the sources). Subjects include data elements, datasets, business processes, systems, and reports. Sources of metadata may be automated, such as schema extraction, system logs, and AI-generated metadata that infers relationships, classifications, and lineage. Other sources are manual, such as glossary entries and policy documents. Recognizing subjects and sources helps stewards clarify what metadata is needed, how it is captured, and how it supports stewardship activities such as quality monitoring, governance, and compliance.

Metadata Lifecycle describes how metadata is created, managed, and used over time. It begins with discovery and definition, followed by collection and storage in repositories and catalogs. Metadata must be kept current, validated, and made accessible for consumption in business and technical processes. Stewards contribute at each stage by promoting metadata creation, supporting quality checks, and encouraging adoption so that metadata becomes a trusted, living resource rather than a static record.

3.2 Metadata Governance

Standards and Conventions establish consistency in how metadata is defined and represented. Naming rules, formatting guidelines, and classification schemes help support metadata that is clear, unambiguous, and consistently represented across systems. For stewards, promoting and applying standards provides a way to reduce confusion, align practices, and improve the usability of metadata as a shared resource.

Metadata Quality focuses on the completeness, accuracy, and reliability of metadata. Incomplete or inconsistent metadata undermines the value of the data it describes, while well-maintained metadata strengthens trust and discoverability. Stewards contribute by reviewing definitions, validating accuracy, and confirming that metadata is kept current as systems and business needs evolve.

Change Management addresses how updates to metadata are introduced, reviewed, and communicated. Definitions, lineage, and classifications often change over time, and unmanaged changes can create confusion or break dependencies. Stewards help coordinate impact analysis, log and track updates, and ensure that downstream users are informed. This stewardship role helps prevent disruption and supports transparency when metadata evolves.

3.3 Metadata Repositories and Tools

Data Catalogs and Business Glossaries make metadata accessible and usable for business and technical audiences. Catalogs help users find and evaluate datasets by providing descriptions, lineage, and usage context. Glossaries define business terms and clarify meanings so that data is interpreted consistently. Stewards encourage adoption of these tools, promote clarity in definitions, and help support catalogs and glossaries that are up to date.

Centralized Metadata Repositories act as system-of-record sources that consolidate metadata from multiple systems into a single, authoritative view. In practice, metadata may originate in different tool-specific catalogs, each tied to specific databases, BI platforms, or cloud services. Central repositories often import and aggregate this metadata to reduce duplication and provide consistency, though challenges remain when organizations must reconcile multiple catalogs. While stewards rarely own these repositories, they play a role in assuring that aggregated metadata is accurate, relevant, and usable across business and technical audiences.

Tool-Specific Stores and Interoperability reflect the reality that metadata is often scattered across systems. Databases, integration platforms, BI tools, cloud services, and individual applications may each generate their own metadata—ranging from catalogs and business glossaries to lineage traces, quality measures, and usage statistics. This proliferation creates overlap and fragmentation, making it difficult to form a complete view. Stewards contribute to interoperability by advocating for alignment across tools, clarifying which sources should be treated as authoritative, and working with technical teams to support appropriate connections or synchronization. Their role is not to engineer integrations, but to define expectations, promote consistency, and confirm that metadata remains discoverable, reliable, and meaningful across a fragmented landscape.

3.4 Metadata Management Architecture

Metadata Management Processes and Products distinguish between the activities that produce metadata and the outcomes that make it usable. Processes include discovery, capture, validation, and enrichment, while products are the catalogs, glossaries, dictionaries, and lineage views that people interact with. For stewards, recognizing this distinction reinforces their dual role: to advocate for strong processes that generate reliable metadata, and for resulting products that are accessible, accurate, and valuable to users.

Metadata Connectivity describes the need for integrated platforms and processes that allow metadata to flow across operational, analytical, and master data systems, as well as quality and observability systems. Connectivity must also extend across deployment models, including multi-cloud, on-premises, and edge environments. Without this integration, metadata remains fragmented and loses value as data moves between systems. Stewards contribute by promoting consistent definitions, advocating interoperability between platforms, and encouraging practices that keep metadata aligned with the data it describes, regardless of where that data resides.

Architectural Challenges for Metadata Management often arise from silos, disparity, and uneven adoption of metadata practices. Multiple catalogs, fragmented repositories, and inconsistent standards can create confusion and erode trust. Self-service tools add complexity when metadata is incomplete or poorly governed. Stewards help address these challenges by advocating for harmonization, communicating about changes, and reinforcing metadata literacy so that users know how to interpret and apply what is available.

FOUR

Data Quality

Data Quality is central to data stewardship because the value of data depends on its fitness for purpose. Poor quality leads to operations errors, flawed analytics, compliance risks, and loss of trust. Stewards do not own all aspects of quality management, but they play a critical role in defining what quality means, clarifying expectations, and guiding quality practices based on business perspectives. By linking quality measures to business use and coordinating the resolution of issues, stewardship helps keep data reliable, usable, and trusted across the organization.

4.1 Data Quality Management Basics

Data Quality Perspectives frame how organizations think about data quality. Data may be judged as defect-free, conforming to specifications, fit for purpose, and meeting customer expectations.

Each perspective highlights different priorities: *defect-free* emphasizes the absence of errors such as missing values, typos, or invalid codes; *specifications* emphasize alignment with the way data was designed, including the rules, structures, and definitions that establish how it should look and behave; *fit for purpose* reflects usability in context, focusing on whether the data supports the task or decision at hand; and *customer expectations* center on business needs, highlighting whether the data delivers the outcomes and level of trust required by stakeholders. Together, these perspectives provide stewards with a multidimensional view of quality that helps them balance competing needs across stakeholders and use cases.

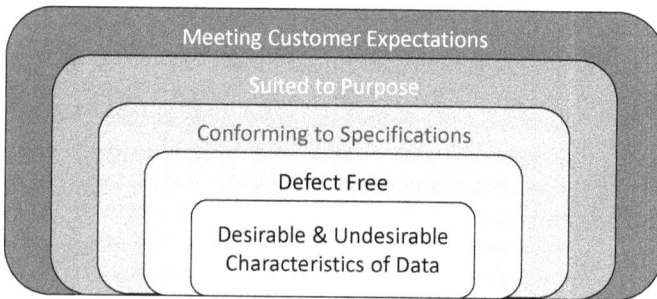

Figure 11: Defining Data Quality.

The ultimate definition of data quality is meeting customer expectations.
To meet customer expectations, data must fit the use case and purpose.
Specifications describe requirements of data use case and purpose.
Specifications express desirable qualities of the data.
Defects are undesirable qualities and absence of desirable qualities.
Evaluating data characteristics is the essence of Data Quality assessment.

Data Quality Practices describe the methods organizations use to manage and improve data quality. Quality control (QC) focuses on inspection and correction, while quality assurance (QA) emphasizes prevention and improvement. Practices such as Total Quality Management, Statistical Process Control, and Six Sigma illustrate how continuous improvement methods from manufacturing and operations have been adapted to information management. Stewards add value by applying these practices to data as well as processes.

4.2 Data Quality Concepts and Principles

Data Quality Core Concepts define what is meant by data quality. At its simplest, quality refers to data that is accurate, complete, and reliable. Expanded definitions add relevance, timeliness, and trustworthiness. These principles highlight that quality is not a single attribute. It is a combination of characteristics that make data usable and credible in context. Clear concepts provide the basis for consistent measurement and management.

Data Defect Causes and Consequences emphasize why quality management matters. Defects often arise from flawed collection processes, erroneous integration and transformation processing, and natural data decay over time. The business consequences can be severe: lost opportunities, reputational damage, regulatory risk, and costly rework. Stewards help surface these consequences and frame quality improvement as both a business and a compliance imperative.

4.3 Data Quality Dimensions

Technical Dimensions of Data Quality focus on data content and structure. Correctness looks checks that data values are accurate, complete, consistent, timely, and recorded at the right level of detail. Integrity checks the structural soundness of data—that it is connected in the right ways, conforms to constraints of values, and is free from unintended dependencies. These dimensions can be measured directly, so they are usually the first focus of quality checks. Stewards help by clarifying expectations so technical checks align with how the business actually uses the data.

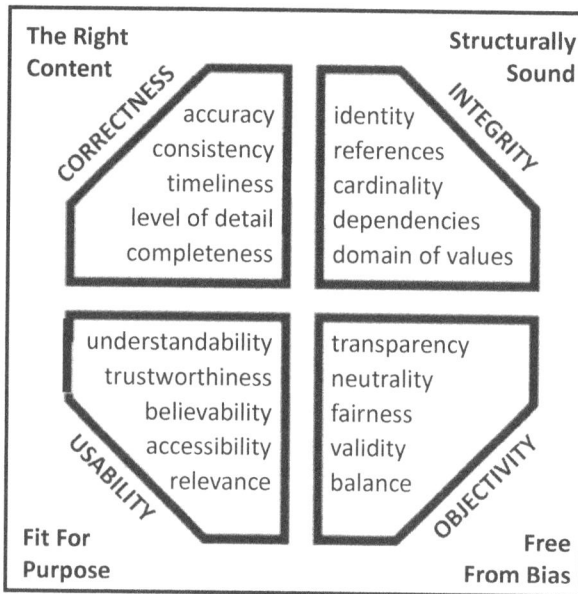

The Right Content	Structurally Sound
CORRECTNESS accuracy consistency timeliness level of detail completeness	INTEGRITY identity references cardinality dependencies domain of values
understandability trustworthiness believability accessibility relevance USABILITY	transparency neutrality fairness validity balance OBJECTIVITY
Fit For Purpose	Free From Bias

Figure 12: Data Quality Dimensions.

Four dimensions and twenty characteristics of data provide a solid foundation for quality assessment and management.

Business and Ethical Dimensions of Data Quality emphasize how data supports use and how it avoids bias. Usability looks at whether data is understandable, trustworthy, accessible, and relevant for the task at hand. Objectivity focuses on the absence of bias and distortion, emphasizing transparency, fairness, validity, and balance. These dimensions are especially important when data influences business decisions or feeds into analytics and AI, where biased or unclear data can cause real harm. By paying attention to both usability and objectivity, stewards extend the view of quality beyond technical measures to also include fairness and practical business impact.

4.4 Data Quality in IT Processes

Data Quality in IT Projects recognizes that many data problems originate in system initiatives: application development, database projects, data conversions, and system migrations. Reviews, validation steps, and controls within projects can prevent quality issues from becoming production problems. Stewards contribute by participating in requirements reviews, validating definitions, and tracing the implementation of data rules. Steward participation helps bridge business expectations with technical execution.

Data Quality by Design in IT projects means building quality methods such as validation rules, quality checkpoints, and observability into applications, databases, and data pipelines from the outset. This is generally considered to be a stronger approach than relying on after-the-fact detection and correction of data quality defects. The "by design" concept is central to this process—addressing quality as a set of requirements that are addressed first in functional design, then carried forward to software development, testing, and deployment. This approach reduces costly rework and makes quality an integral part of development and implementation processes. Stewards advocate for quality by design by influencing project practices and openly expressing the need for quality requirements to be an integral part of design. Data steward advocacy shapes culture so projects deliver functional systems and data that is trusted, traceable, and of high quality.

4.5 Data Quality for Structured Data

Quality Assurance for Structured Data benefits from the explicit rules and constraints built into relational data models and databases. Integrity rules, such as identity, reference, cardinality, and value set constraints, are often directly visible in the data model and may be enforced systematically by the database. These rules help support uniqueness, prevent "orphan" records, and keep data values within valid domains. Correctness, although less visible than integrity in data models, is strongly supported by mature profiling tools that can assess accuracy, completeness, and consistency. Profiling also highlights skew, outliers, and completeness gaps, which can reveal hidden bias or other quality risks. Although structured environments offer strong support for monitoring and validation, issues such as duplicates, outdated values, or poorly defined rules can still arise. Stewards contribute by validating that data quality rules align with business rules, and by verifying that data quality checks are built into processes that collect and maintain data.

Quality Control for Structured Data focuses on monitoring to detect, correct, and prevent the recurrence of issues that elude quality assurance checks. Even with strong schema enforcement, errors such as duplicate records, misapplied codes, or outdated values may occur. Control activities include routine profiling, exception reporting, and remediation processes to correct errors and prevent them from propagating across systems and databases. Root cause analysis is a crucial element that helps identify where problems originate and puts safeguards in place to prevent repeated occurrences. Stewards support these efforts by prioritizing defect resolution efforts, coordinating resolution activities with data owners, and documenting corrective actions.

4.6 Data Quality for Semi-Structured Data

Quality Assurance for Semi-Structured Data addresses environments where data has some structure but without a rigid schema—data formats such as JSON, XML, and event streams. Assurance activities include monitoring schema evolution, validating against registries, and applying formatting and structural standards. Integrity is a frequent concern, as schema drift can break dependencies or make data inconsistent across sources. Correctness is supported through profiling that identifies missing fields, unexpected values, and irregular nesting patterns. Usability comes into play when naming and structuring conventions influence the ease or difficulty of interpreting and understanding data. To check objectivity in semi-structured formats, profiling reveals skew and imbalance in captured attributes. Stewards contribute by defining expectations for how fields should be captured and by confirming that evolving structures remain consistent with business meaning.

Quality Control for Semi-Structured Data focuses on catching and correcting issues that assurance cannot prevent. Common problems include malformed records, inconsistent tags, and incomplete event streams. Control activities include profiling, exception handling, and transformation logic to repair or reformat problematic data. Root cause analysis is often needed to identify whether issues originate from upstream systems or manual entry processes. Stewards help prioritize which issues matter, work with system owners to remediate recurring problems, and document correction rules for reuse.

4.7 Data Quality for Unstructured Data

Quality Assurance for Unstructured Data focuses on making text, images, video, and audio workable and interpretable by introducing structure through metadata, classification, and labeling. Correctness is supported when labels and tags accurately describe content; integrity depends on consistent application of labeling schemes across collections. Usability is addressed by addressing clarity, coherence, and readability so that unstructured data can be reliably interpreted. Objectivity becomes a central concern, as labeling and classification are prone to human or algorithmic bias. Assurance practices include guidelines and validation steps to reduce unfair or unrepresentative results. Stewards advocate for metadata standards, monitor labeling quality, and encourage practices that preserve both accuracy and fairness in unstructured data assets.

Quality Control for Unstructured Data addresses problems that assurance cannot prevent, such as transcription errors, mislabeled images, poor-quality recordings, and noisy datasets. Control activities include cleansing, enrichment, re-labeling, and filtering to improve correctness and usability, while also checking that integrity is preserved across related datasets. Objectivity is again a concern, as biased or inconsistent corrections can amplify problems rather than resolve them. Stewards support these activities by helping define acceptable thresholds for unstructured data quality, aligning corrections with intended business use, and monitoring for recurring issues that require upstream improvements.

4.8 Measuring and Managing Data Quality

Data Quality Metrics and Measures provide a structured way to evaluate correctness, integrity, usability, and objectivity. Measures are specific observations such as counts of missing values, broken references, late arrivals, and skew in population representation. Metrics aggregate or summarize these measures, turning them into percentages, indexes, or scores that can be tracked and compared over time. Together, they make quality tangible and visible. Stewards play a key role by helping define what should be measured, confirming that metrics reflect business priorities, and validating that results are meaningful in the context of how data is actually used.

Data Quality Management applies data quality metrics and measures in ongoing practice. Organizations use dashboards, scorecards, and monitoring frameworks to observe trends, track progress, and identify emerging issues. Metrics help prioritize where corrective action is needed, guide planning for remediation or improvement, and monitor whether changes are effective over time. Stewards contribute by interpreting results, coordinating with stakeholders to address problems, and advocating for processes that prevent defects from recurring. Their involvement supports measurement that is a practical driver of continuous quality improvement.

FIVE

Data Stewardship Processes

Data Stewardship Processes are the activities where stewardship responsibilities are most visible in daily practice. These processes connect data needs with data capabilities by applying definitions, quality, policies, protection, and collaboration in everyday data management. They highlight the steward's role in guiding practices for data that is well-documented, meets business expectations for quality, is protected and compliant, and is supported by policies and cultural adoption. Together, these processes show how stewards translate governance principles into action and address the practical challenges of working with data.

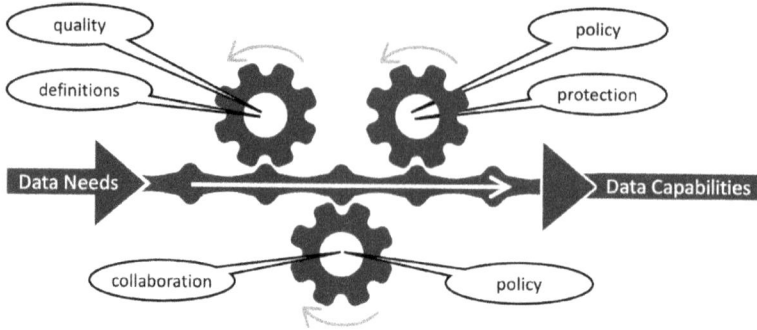

Figure 13: Processes Driving Capabilities.

Stewardship processes connect data needs with data capabilities by applying definitions, quality, policies, protection, and collaboration in day-to-day data management practices.

5.1 Data Definition and Quality

Metadata Stewardship focuses on the definitions, descriptions, and context that make data understandable and usable. Stewards confirm that business terms, data elements, and valid values are defined clearly and used consistently. Beyond definitional metadata, they address quality by documenting lineage to show origins, transformations, and usage. They maintain catalogs and glossaries to keep metadata accessible, apply conventions for naming and classification, and capture rules, quality expectations, and sensitivity levels as metadata. Stewardship also includes managing changes to metadata and promoting literacy so stakeholders can effectively use catalogs and lineage tools.

Data Quality Stewardship focuses on defining what quality means for data and establishing clear expectations that are documented and applied consistently. Because data serves many purposes, what is considered "fit for purpose" may vary by use case, and stewards help balance these differences by working with stakeholders to agree on rules and thresholds. They also help prioritize issues based on business impact and coordinate resolution when defects arise. Their role is to connect business needs with data quality practices, making sure that quality measures reflect how data is actually used in operations, reporting, and compliance. By clarifying expectations and guiding remediation, stewards support data management efforts that deliver outcomes the business can trust.

5.2 Policy and Protection

Data Policy Stewardship supports practical and effective creation, maintenance, and application of data governance policies. Policies are a shared responsibility. Data governance provides the authority and accountability to define and approve them. Data stewardship drives practical adoption by translating policies into everyday practices and guiding people in their consistent use. Stewards contribute to policymaking by identifying needs, analyzing implications, consulting stakeholders, and drafting policies that are clear and actionable. Their role extends to maintaining policies over time—reviewing for relevance, monitoring regulatory changes, and documenting updates—so that policies remain aligned with business and compliance requirements. Stewards also support compliance by providing guides, guardrails, and gates that help people understand policies, prevent mistakes, and block violations when necessary. Data policy stewardship turns governance principles into usable rules that guide day-to-day practice.

Data Protection Stewardship works to safeguard data against misuse, corruption, loss, and unauthorized access, while embedding privacy and security into everyday data practices. Stewards help classify sensitive data, apply protective labels, and review access authorizations. They coordinate secure disposal at the end of data lifecycles, support audits, and assist in incident response when security issues arise. Stewards also play a proactive role in fostering a culture of protection, promoting privacy by design and default, and encouraging all stakeholders to take protective responsibilities seriously. In partnership with IT, security, and governance teams, stewards help to translate protection requirements into action.

5.3 Collaboration and Culture

Issue Resolution Stewardship focuses on data problem identification, tracking, and resolution. Stewards often serve as the first point of contact when data issues arise, logging problems, clarifying symptoms, and helping trace root causes. They frequently lead problem-solving efforts, applying facilitation skills to bring the right people together and guide them toward resolution. Their role goes beyond support for corrective actions to include highlighting, documenting, and sharing lessons learned in a way that helps to reduce the probability of repeated issues. Effective issue stewardship builds trust by showing that problems are addressed systematically and collaboratively.

Data Literacy Stewardship helps people to understand, interpret, and use data appropriately. Stewards act as guides and coaches, helping colleagues grasp definitions, lineage, and quality considerations, while also advocating for accessible tools and training that promote responsible use. Data literacy stewardship extends beyond answering questions by fostering curiosity, demonstrating good practices, and cultivating confidence in working with data. By promoting literacy, stewards help reduce misunderstandings, bridge gaps between business and technical teams, and strengthen collaboration across the organization.

Data Culture Stewardship promotes attitudes, values, and shared practices that influence how an organization interacts with data. Stewards advocate for treating data as an asset, encouraging collaboration, discouraging territorialism, and fostering transparency and trust. They also promote data-informed decision making, encouraging leaders and teams to routinely rely on data as a key part of their choices. This connects closely with literacy, since decision makers must know how to inform themselves with data to use it effectively. Culture stewardship is as much about advocacy as it is about action—stewards lead by example, demonstrating the mindset and habits that build a strong, data-aware culture.

SIX

Data Governance

Data Governance establishes the authority, decision rights, and accountability structures that guide how data is defined, managed, and used. It provides the framework to align policies, standards, and responsibilities with organizational goals, balancing the need for compliance and protection with the drive for business value. For stewards, governance is both the source of direction and the environment within which they operate. By connecting authority with practice, governance and stewardship together position data as a managed, trusted, and shared organizational resource.

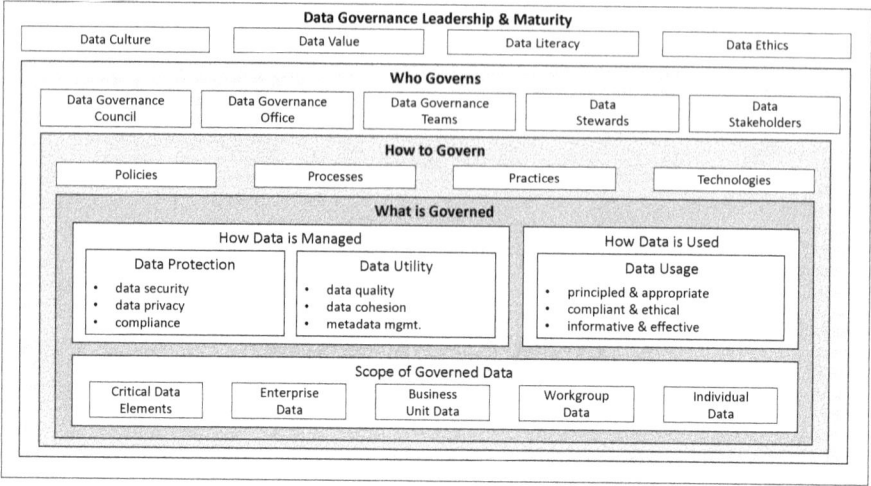

Figure 14: The Data Governance Framework.

The Data Governance Framework illustrates how governance guides the management and use of data. It illustrates roles and methods, aspects of data that are governed, and the governed data. People, policies, practices, and processes all work together for good governance.

6.1 Data Governance Basics

Purpose and Goals of Data Governance center on managing data so that it is available, usable, consistent, protected, and used to create value. Governance establishes the authority to define how data should be managed and used, setting expectations that balance business needs, compliance requirements, and risk considerations. For stewards, these goals provide the framework within which their day-to-day activities operate—a model for stewardship that aligns with organizational priorities and delivers outcomes that matter.

Data Governance versus Data Management highlights an important distinction between setting direction and carrying out practices. Data governance defines rules, assigns responsibilities, and establishes accountability. Data management implements processes and technologies to meet the governance requirements. Data governance decides what standards should exist. Data management applies the standards through design, quality monitoring, integration, and protection activities. Stewards need to understand this distinction because they often operate at the boundary—translating governance decisions into management practices and feeding back operational realities into governance discussions.

Governance and Stewardship are closely related but not identical. Governance is about authority, decision rights, and oversight, while stewardship is about responsibility, collaboration, and execution within those boundaries. Both share the goal of managing data that is trustworthy and responsibly used. Governance provides the policies and frameworks; stewardship helps those policies be understood, adopted in practice, and adapted where necessary to fit real business and data management contexts. Seeing governance and stewardship as complementary clarifies roles: governance sets the "what" and "why," stewardship carries out the "how," and together they sustain a coherent, accountable approach to managing data.

6.2 Scope of Governance

What Data to Govern reflects the fact that governance applies across multiple contexts, from enterprise-wide policies to department-specific practices. At the highest level, enterprise governance sets standards for critical and shared data. Business unit and workgroup levels address domain-specific needs, while individual users and third-party partners also play roles in creating and consuming governed data. For stewards, understanding these levels is important because stewardship responsibilities often extend across boundaries, requiring collaboration to align local practices with enterprise expectations.

Critical and Sensitive Data demand particular attention because of their impact and risk. Critical data elements (CDEs), master data, and reference data drive key business processes, while sensitive data such as personally identifiable information (PII) and compliance-regulated content carry legal and ethical obligations. Governance defines how these categories are identified, prioritized, and controlled. Stewards support these efforts by clarifying definitions, documenting lineage, and helping monitor adherence to policies that safeguard both business value and regulatory compliance.

6.3 Policy Management

Policy Making begins when the need for a new policy is identified—whether to close a regulatory gap, resolve inconsistencies in practice, or clarify standards. Governance bodies provide the authority to approve policies, while stewards play a key role in shaping them. They research context, gather input from stakeholders, and help draft language that defines purpose, scope, and responsibilities in clear, practical terms. Stewards also facilitate review and feedback, shaping policies are understood and workable before they are finalized. Their involvement helps bridge governance intent with business and technical realities.

Policy Lifecycle covers the progression of policies from creation to retirement. Once adopted, policies must be reviewed regularly, updated to reflect changes in requirements, and eventually retired when they no longer serve a purpose. Governance councils provide oversight, while stewards support the lifecycle by maintaining change history, documenting rationale, and helping communicate revisions. This ongoing management helps to keep policies relevant, traceable, and practical to apply.

Policy Maintenance emphasizes the work of keeping policies effective over time. This includes monitoring external changes in laws, regulations, and standards, evaluating whether policies cover current needs, and conducting gap analyses to spot weaknesses. Stewards bring forward feedback from data stakeholders, helping to refine clarity and applicability. Stewards help maintain alignment between governance expectations and organizational practice by promoting continuous improvement.

Policy Compliance is the work of moving policies from paper into practice. Compliance mechanisms can be thought of as guides, guardrails, and gates: guides clarify expectations and explain how to comply, guardrails steer people toward correct actions, and gates enforce restrictions through controls such as authentication and access limits. Stewards contribute at every layer, from drafting guides to supporting workflow design and monitoring compliance activities. Their role helps to make compliance feel more like enablement than enforcement—more like partnering than policing—building a culture where policies are both understood and consistently followed.

6.4 Governance Roles and Responsibilities

Decision Rights and Accountability define who has the authority to make governance decisions and who is responsible for outcomes. Governance councils, data owners, custodians, and stewards each have different roles in shaping and applying policies. Clear decision rights prevent ambiguity, reduce conflict, and establish accountability when issues arise. Stewards play a key part by clarifying roles, facilitating alignment, and making sure that governance decisions are informed by practical realities of data use.

Collaboration and Engagement emphasize that governance is not the work of a single group but a collective responsibility across business, IT, compliance, and other functions. Effective governance depends on broad participation and ongoing dialogue to balance priorities and resolve conflicts. Stewards often act as connectors, bridging perspectives between business stakeholders and technical teams, and facilitating governance decisions that are actionable and supported. Their ability to foster collaboration strengthens governance by building shared ownership and trust.

6.5 Data Governance Processes

Core Governance Processes define how data-related authority and accountability operate within an organization. These include establishing policies, setting standards, assigning decision rights, and monitoring compliance. Governance also provides the framework for issue escalation, providing the mechanisms to be sure that problems are logged, evaluated, and addressed through the right channels. In some cases, this extends to incident oversight, where governance defines how incidents are reported, who is accountable, and what corrective actions are required— even when the response itself belongs to other functions such as IT or security. For stewards, familiarity with these core processes is essential because they often serve as participants, facilitators, or advocates within them.

Execution of Governance describes how governance decisions move from policy to practice. Governance sets expectations, but those expectations are only realized when they are implemented through data management activities such as quality monitoring, metadata maintenance, and protection controls. Stewards frequently operate at this boundary, translating governance language into actionable rules, supporting the adoption of these rules in business processes, and providing feedback when execution reveals conflicts or gaps. By linking high-level authority with everyday practice, stewardship helps to make governance more than aspiration—it becomes an operational reality.

6.6 Data Governance and Enterprise Governance

Alignment with Other Governance Domains recognizes that data governance is part of a larger governance landscape. Corporate governance establishes overall accountability to stakeholders, while IT governance focuses on technology priorities and risks, and compliance governance addresses legal and regulatory requirements. Data governance must align with all of these, establishing data policies and practices that support enterprise objectives. Stewards contribute by maintaining visibility into these broader domains and helping to confirm that data-related decisions reinforce and do not conflict with enterprise governance priorities.

Interdependence with Adjacent Disciplines reflects the reality that governance decisions about data influence and are influenced by many other areas of practice. Analytics and AI/ML depend on governed data to produce trustworthy results. Security and risk management rely on governance frameworks to define classification, access, and protection requirements. Architecture disciplines—business, data, systems, and technology—are equally interdependent, since governance sets the rules for consistency and accountability, while architecture provides the structures through which those rules are implemented. Business process management, customer experience, and operational efficiency are also directly affected by governance choices. Stewards help to connect these disciplines by articulating data needs, clarifying policies, and fostering collaboration across functional boundaries.

6.7 Leadership and Maturity

Governance Leadership provides the authority and sponsorship necessary for governance to succeed. Executive sponsors, such as a CDO, CIO, or senior business leaders, signal the importance of governance and secure resources to sustain it. Councils and committees provide forums for decision-making, while data owners exercise authority within their domains, making decisions about definitions, standards, and usage. Stewards support leadership by bringing forward operational realities, facilitating dialogue, and helping leaders balance governance goals with practical constraints. Without visible leadership, governance risks being perceived as optional rather than essential.

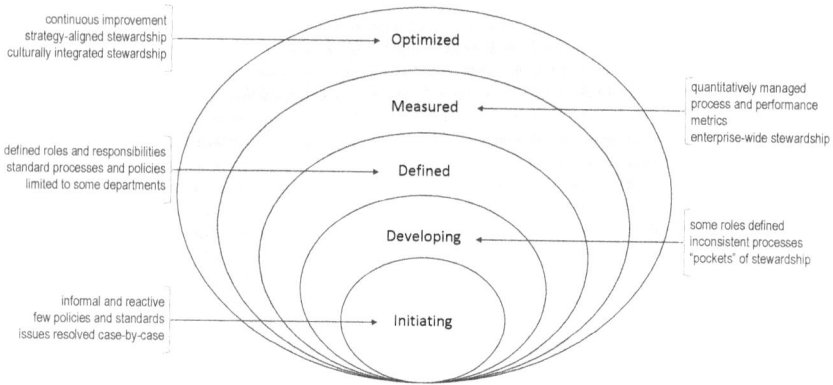

Figure 15: Data Governance Maturity Model.

Five stages of governance maturity
from ad hoc to culturally embedded data practices.

Governance Maturity describes how governance capabilities evolve from informal and ad hoc practices to a structured, embedded program. Early stages often rely on isolated efforts or individual champions, while higher maturity levels are characterized by formal councils, documented processes, and integration into enterprise governance. At full maturity, governance is part of the organizational culture, with policies and practices applied consistently and understood broadly. Stewards contribute to this evolution by advocating for adoption, participating in assessments, and modeling good practices that help governance progress from concept to embedded discipline.

SEVEN

Data Management Processes

Data Management Processes are the activities and practices that guide how data is handled throughout its lifecycle. Data stewards engage with these activities to understand management practices, advocate for improvements, and address issues related to data quality, protection, compliance, and other stewardship concerns. Stewardship is closely tied to the way data is structured and managed, with these activities providing the practical framework through which responsibilities are carried out. They include efforts to establish shared meaning, maintain quality, integrate data across systems, and support access and understanding. By aligning stewardship with data management, organizations help make sure that accountability is embedded where data is created, transformed, and used.

7.1 Data Design and Quality

Naming Data involves establishing clear, consistent names for data objects—entities, files, tables, columns, fields, etc.—that reflect meaning, content, and usage. Carefully-chosen names reduce ambiguity and improve communication between business and technical teams. Naming standards support data objects that are identifiable, easily understood, and used consistently across systems and processes. This process is fundamental to building a shared understanding of data within the organization.

Defining Data establishes agreed meanings and descriptions for data elements so they can be consistently interpreted and applied. Clear definitions reduce ambiguity, support compliance with policies and standards, and enable alignment between business and technical perspectives. Clear, well-structured definitions follow a pattern of "tell me what it is, tell me what it isn't, and give me an example." The data definition process is a core element of data stewardship, building the foundation for everyone working with the data to be working from the same understanding.

Designing Data determines how data elements and datasets are organized and structured to work together in systems and processes. Good design establishes clear relationships, minimizes redundancy, and structures data to be stored, retrieved, and maintained effectively, while also supporting both business and technical needs. Design should anticipate future use, creating data that can adapt as requirements change. Stewards contribute to design by bringing business meaning, context, and expectations into the process in ways that help to shape structures that make data understandable, usable, and trustworthy across its lifecycle.

Managing Data Quality supports data that meets expectations for correctness, integrity, usability, and objectivity. Quality management combines quality control and quality assurance within a framework of measurement and monitoring. Control activities detect and correct data quality defects. Assurance activities set expectations and put processes in place to prevent defects. Monitoring focuses on problems such as missing values, inconsistent formats, inaccurate records, ambiguous presentation, and data bias, providing the evidence needed for both assurance and control. Stewardship contributes by making expectations explicit, documenting rules, and coordinating resolutions when problems arise. The management of data quality is a key responsibility of stewardship because deficiencies can have far-reaching and severe impacts.

Connecting and Integrating Data brings together information from different sources so that data can be used consistently and effectively. Integration involves resolving differences in structure, semantics, and quality, and aligning the combined data with business meaning. Methods may include transformation, mapping, or linking, depending on how closely the sources must be connected. Data interoperability connects data by linking based on business context and semantics. Stewardship contributes by clarifying definitions, identifying potential conflicts, and confirming that integration and interoperability outcomes support both business and technical needs. Effective interconnection of data is critical because organizations depend on data that spans systems, processes, and domains.

7.2 Data Storage and Access

Accessing Data addresses the processes and mechanisms for people and systems to find, connect with, and retrieve data. Effective access balances availability with control, supporting data that is easy to find and acquire by those who need it, while protecting it from unauthorized use. Access processes may include authentication, authorization, and permission management, as well as mechanisms for search and discovery. Stewardship contributes by helping define who should have access, under what conditions, and for what purposes. Properly managed access ensures that data is available for appropriate use but also safeguarded from loss, damage, and misuse.

Managing Metadata involves capturing, organizing, and maintaining information that describes data. Metadata provides context by recording definitions, classifications, structures, and lineage. Managed metadata makes data easier to find, understand, and use. It also supports governance by documenting rules, ownership, and responsibilities. Well-managed metadata can automate aspects of data management and governance, such as applying security classifications, enforcing retention rules, and tracing data lineage for impact analysis. Effective metadata management improves discoverability, strengthens trust, and enables compliance with regulatory requirements. Stewardship plays a key role in supporting metadata accuracy, completeness, and accessibility.

Managing Databases involves overseeing how data is stored, organized, and made available through database platforms. This work spans schema design and maintenance, performance and scalability management, security and availability management, and backup, recovery, and version control to protect data assets. From a stewardship perspective, database management is important because it directly affects accessibility, consistency, and trustworthiness of data for business use.

Managing Systems focuses on the broader applications and platforms that process, move, and deliver data. This includes transaction systems, data warehouses, data lakes, and analytical platforms, as well as the pipelines and workflows that connect them. Key concerns include performance, scalability, security, and availability. For stewardship, system management matters because system management issues are often the root cause of data issues—inconsistent integrations, missing and delayed data, availability and access failures, and similar problems—while well-managed systems reduce the frequency of problems and improve the sustainability and usability of data.

Governing Data establishes the rules, policies, and decision rights that guide how data is managed and used. Governance includes responsibilities, accountabilities, and standards for definitions, quality, access, protection, and compliance. Governance provides the authority that enables stewardship to function, giving stewards a framework to address issues and promote consistency of data practices across the organization. Effective governance promotes data that is managed as a shared asset, balancing business value, regulatory requirements, and ethical considerations.

Protecting Data encompasses the practices and processes to safeguard data and information against corruption, loss, misuse, and unauthorized access. Protection measures include access controls, encryption, backup and recovery, and monitoring for security threats. Stewardship connects to protection by clarifying data classifications, defining sensitivity levels, and establishing controls that match business requirements. Effective protection maintains trust, meets regulatory obligations, and prevents harm that could result from breaches and misuse.

7.3 Data Creation and Consumption

Capturing Operational Data involves recording the information created in the course of day-to-day business activities. Most of this data originates from transactional systems, such as order entry, billing, inventory, or customer service. Other sources of operational data include workflow automation, manufacturing systems, equipment monitors, and IoT devices that track conditions in real-time. Stewardship focuses on definition and quality at the point of data capture, and prevention of error propagation to downstream processes.

Operational Reporting and Analysis uses data to track and manage day-to-day business activities. Reports and dashboards provide visibility into current operations, monitor performance against targets, and surface exceptions that need immediate action. Operational analytics applies similar techniques in real-time, supporting direct actions within business processes. Examples include fraud detection in financial transactions, predictive maintenance alerts from IoT sensors, and customer service dashboards that guide immediate responses. Stewardship supports these uses by supporting operational data that is accurate, consistent, and aligned with business definitions. Reliable data supports frontline decisions and rapid responses that are based on trustworthy information.

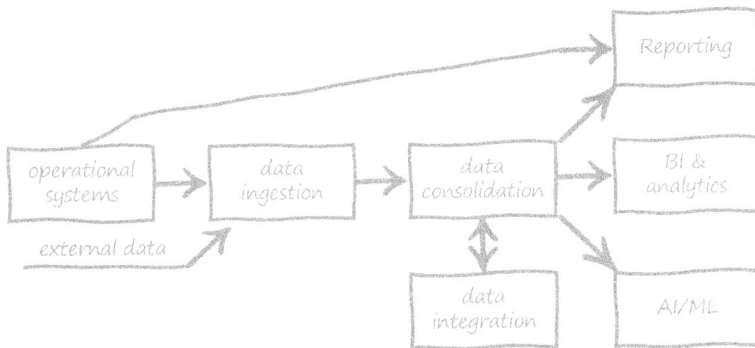

Figure 16: Creation and Consumption – The Data Lifecycle.

Data flows through a series of processes and serves a variety of operational and analytical use cases. Data stewards advocate and support good data practices throughout the lifecycle.

Managing Analytical Data involves organizing and controlling data that is prepared for reporting, analysis, forecasting, prediction, and advanced use cases such as AI and machine learning. The lifecycle begins with ingestion from operational and external sources, continues through transformation and storage in analytical databases, and extends to consumption in reports, dashboards, models, and applications. Each stage requires attention to quality and consistency to deliver reliable results, as well as to security and compliance, to protect sensitive information and meet regulatory obligations. Stewardship contributes by clarifying definitions, monitoring quality, and connecting data used for analysis to its original meaning and context. Stewards also help define access controls, apply protection requirements, and confirm that analytical data practices follow organizational and regulatory policies.

Preparing Data for Analysis involves transforming raw data into forms that are clean, consistent, and suitable for use in reports, dashboards, and analytic models. Preparation activities may include profiling, cleansing, standardizing, enriching, and joining data from multiple sources. The goal is to reduce noise, resolve inconsistencies, and improve usability, allowing analysts and modelers to focus on insights rather than cleanup. Stewardship contributes by documenting preparation rules, reinforcing alignment with business definitions, and verifying that preparation practices preserve meaning and context. Good data preparation improves efficiency, increases confidence in analytical outcomes, and reduces the risk of errors in decision-making.

Data Products are thoughtfully designed collections of data that include the data itself, packaged together with the processing, rules, and context needed to use it effectively. They often provide access through interfaces like APIs or dashboards, helping people and systems consume the data reliably and consistently. Unlike raw data sets, data products come with built-in quality controls, documentation, and metadata that explain what the data means and how it should be used. Stewards help shape the culture around data products by defining clear ownership, promoting transparency, and fostering compliance with quality and privacy standards. By guiding data product creation and responsible use, stewards foster trust and enable ongoing value from data sharing across the organization.

Analytical Reporting and Analysis processes use data to explore trends, measure performance, and support decision-making. Business intelligence (BI) tools provide the platforms for reports, dashboards, and queries that summarize information for business leaders and operational managers. Beyond reporting, analysis identifies patterns, correlations, and drivers of outcomes. Advanced techniques may include forecasting, scenario modeling, and statistical analysis to guide strategic choices. Stewardship contributes by supporting data used in BI and analytical work that is well-defined, consistent across reports, and interpreted with the right business context. Clear stewardship reduces conflicting results and strengthens confidence in analytical findings.

Artificial intelligence (AI) and Machine Learning (ML) apply advanced methods to discover patterns, generate predictions, and automate decisions. Leading-edge developments, such as generative AI and agentic AI, extend these processes with capabilities to create new content, simulate environments, and enable systems to act with a degree of autonomy. These uses depend on analytical data that is well-prepared, structured, and governed to support training, validation, and monitoring. Stewardship plays a critical role by reinforcing expectations that data used in AI and ML is accurate, complete, and representative, by documenting lineage for transparency, and by monitoring for bias, compliance, and responsible application of results.

EIGHT

Data Integration and Interoperability

Data Integration and Interoperability describe two ways of connecting data across systems. Data integration copies and transforms data to consolidate it into shared data stores that provide a unified view for reporting, analytics, and advanced use cases. Data interoperability enables systems to exchange and interpret data directly, avoiding the need to create new copies. Both approaches are important: integration provides persistence, history, and centralized control, while interoperability supports timeliness, flexibility, and cross-system continuity. Both approaches are challenged by systems with inconsistent names, definitions, and encodings—each with its own semantics, schema, and conventions. Stewards contribute to integration and interoperability by clarifying definitions, promoting consistency in meaning, and supporting quality practices so that connected data can be trusted and used consistently across the organization.

8.1 Data Integration

Data Integration Processes involve moving and consolidating data from multiple sources into a common form. Techniques such as ETL (extract, transform, load), ELT (extract, load, transform), and replication are widely used to create centralized stores like warehouses or lakes. These methods allow data from diverse operational systems to be combined into a consistent structure.

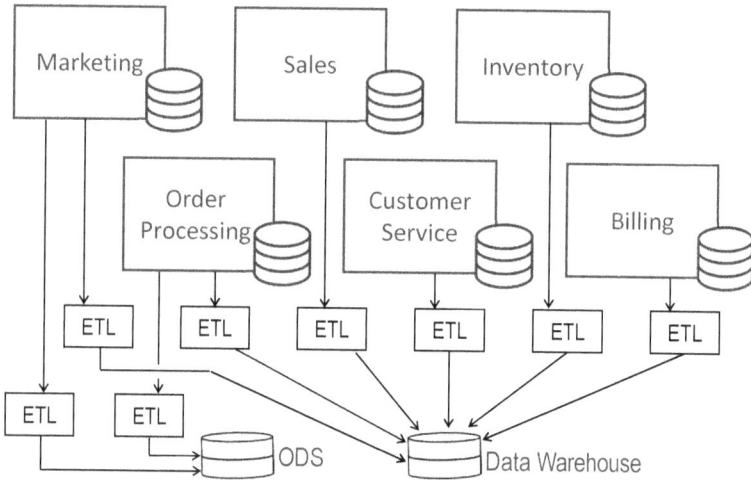

Figure 17: Data Integration Architecture.

Data equivalence prescribed by target schema.
Data translations built into ETL processing.
Data copies raise data lineage questions.

Data Integration Benefits include support for reporting, analytics, compliance, and regulatory oversight. Without integration, it can be difficult to form a comprehensive view of an organization's data, especially across disparate applications, platforms, and points in time. Integrated data stores typically retain historical data that may no longer exist in source systems. This provides data that is essential for time-based analysis. Historical data enables organizations to examine long-term trends, conduct year-over-year comparisons, perform time-series forecasting, and meet audit and regulatory requirements that depend on a complete record of past activity. Without integration, it would be difficult to form a comprehensive view of the organization's data, especially across disparate applications and platforms.

Data Integration Stewardship focuses on how integration affects definitions, quality, and usability. Transformations applied during integration can change the meaning of data, requiring stewards to ensure that business definitions remain clear and that mappings are documented. Integration may also introduce timeliness issues, since consolidated data often lags behind operational sources. Stewards contribute by clarifying compromises made in schema alignment, documenting quality expectations, and helping users interpret integrated data appropriately.

8.2 Data Interoperability

Data Interoperability Methods focus on enabling systems to exchange and interpret data without creating new copies. Instead of consolidating data into a central store, interoperability relies on shared semantics, consistent definitions, and agreed-upon conventions for data representation. Mapping disparate data to a shared business context and common semantics provides the foundation for interoperability. Building on that foundation, standard interfaces and semantic layers enable systems to interact directly with a clear and consistent understanding of data meanings.

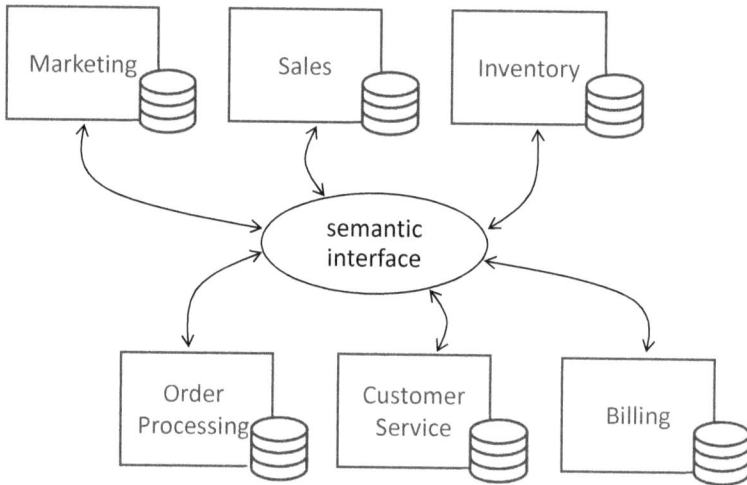

Figure 18: Semantic Data Interoperability.

Data equivalence based on semantic layer.
Data translations local to each system.
Copies minimized and data sharing simplified.

Data Interoperability Benefits include timeliness, flexibility, and continuity across environments. Because data does not need to be moved or replicated, it can be used in near real time to support a continuum of use cases from operational needs to advanced analytics. Interoperability reduces reliance on large-scale data consolidation, making it practical to connect new systems and data without compromising consistency of meaning.

Data Interoperability Stewardship focuses on the role of stewards in clarifying definitions, documenting metadata, and advocating for consistent practices. Unlike integration, where transformations are applied during data movement, interoperability depends on alignment of meaning before data is exchanged. Stewards help by assuring that definitions are unambiguous, business rules are documented, and stakeholders share a common understanding. Their work makes interoperability practical by reducing the risks of misinterpretation across systems and domains.

8.3 Comparing Integration and Interoperability

Differences Between Integration and Interoperability center on how data is connected and used. Integration depends on copy-based movement into centralized stores, with structural transformations to achieve alignment. Interoperability avoids copying by enabling systems to interpret cross-domain data directly, relying on semantic consistency rather than schema compromises. Both approaches serve the goal of making data usable, but they achieve it in different ways.

Benefits and Limitations need to be understood to make informed decisions about when to use each approach. Integration provides persistence, history, and centralized control, making it reliable for analytics and compliance, but it can add additional stored copies of data, introduce latency, and increase complexity. Interoperability offers timeliness and flexibility, but it depends on agreement about meaning and can be difficult to achieve across diverse systems. Most organizations need both: integration for long-term storage and oversight, and interoperability for agility and cross-system continuity.

The Stewardship Role is to help the organization apply each approach appropriately and reduce confusion when both are in play. Stewards contribute by documenting definitions, clarifying transformation rules, and making integration compromises. For interoperability, they support shared semantics, metadata alignment, and cross-domain understanding. A stewardship perspective helps balance the strengths and challenges of both approaches, supporting practices for data that is used effectively regardless of how it is connected.

NINE

Data Culture

Data Culture is the mindset, behaviors, and shared practices that shape how people and organizations engage with data. It influences whether data is trusted, how it is applied in decisions, and the degree to which data is treated as a shared asset. For stewards, data culture is both context and opportunity: they work within existing norms while also helping to shift them toward greater literacy, responsibility, and adoption. The key elements of data culture include developing capabilities at both the individual and organizational level, fostering literacy that equips people to use data confidently, embedding ethical principles that guide responsible choices, and encouraging orientation and adoption so that data becomes part of everyday work. Together, these elements establish how deeply data is integrated into the fabric of the organization and how effectively it supports decision-making.

9.1 Data Capabilities

Knowledge Worker Capabilities are the skills and practices that people apply when creating, using, and interpreting data in their daily activities. Sales staff, customer service representatives, human resource (HR) specialists, and others both generate operational data through their work and rely on reports, dashboards, or records to monitor performance, guide tasks, and support customer interactions. The most important capabilities for this group include recording data accurately, reading displays with understanding, interpreting metrics in context, and knowing when to ask questions or seek clarification. For stewards, supporting knowledge workers often means promoting clarity in definitions, reducing ambiguity in reports, and helping to capture and present in ways that are accessible, accurate, and usable.

Decision Maker Capabilities are the skills and practices that managers and leaders apply when engaging with data. They shape the demand for data by asking questions, framing problems, and defining measures that guide management decisions. As consumers of data, they rely on reports, dashboards, and analyses to evaluate options, set priorities, predict results, and track outcomes. To work with data effectively, they need capabilities to interpret data responsibly, recognize limitations such as timeliness, bias, and incomplete coverage, and balance quantitative insights with sound business judgment. They also need to probe reliability, assess transparency, and challenge assumptions to be confident that the data and analyses they use are trustworthy. Stewards support decision makers by clarifying meaning, documenting lineage and quality considerations, and reinforcing data-informed decision making as a normal part of leadership practice.

Business and Data Analyst Capabilities are the skills and practices that enable analysts to use existing data, to discover patterns and create analyses, and to present information in new forms. Analysts locate and combine data across systems, apply transformations and quality checks, and use analytic techniques to identify patterns and build models. They also develop metrics, visualizations, and reports that communicate findings and guide action. Their capabilities include exploring and analyzing data to identify patterns and relationships, applying quality checks, interpreting results responsibly, developing visualizations that communicate effectively, and presenting conclusions in clear and usable ways. Stewards support analysts by helping maintain reliable metadata, clarifying rules and definitions, and reducing the risk of misinterpretation when data is drawn from multiple sources.

Organizational Capabilities are the collective effects of many individual capabilities—capabilities of knowledge workers, decision makers, data analysts, data owners, data stewards, data governors, data architects, data engineers, and many more roles. Combined with shared structures and resources, these individual capabilities create a data-capable organization. Governance frameworks, policies, metadata repositories, data catalogs, and quality dashboards provide the foundation. The diverse data-related roles apply their skills to put the resources into practice. Stewards fill a connecting role by linking organizational resources with individual needs, helping individuals to develop literacy, and providing feedback that strengthens shared capabilities over time.

9.2 Data Literacy

Data-Literate Data Stewards demonstrate the ability to understand, interpret, and communicate data concepts with clarity. They are comfortable with definitions, quality dimensions, and lineage, and they can translate between technical and business language. Being data literate also means recognizing the limitations of data, asking critical questions about its accuracy or completeness, and explaining those limitations in a way others can understand. For stewards, literacy extends beyond their own competence to also serve as role models for responsible data use.

Developing Individual Data Literacy is an important part of stewardship. Stewards support many roles—knowledge workers who read reports, business analysts who explore and interpret data, decision makers who frame questions and express data needs, and data owners who require a broad understanding of data resources. They provide coaching and mentoring through formal training, informal guidance, and practical reference tools, helping people build confidence to use data responsibly without needing to be experts. Stewards also continue to build their own literacy, deepening both general data knowledge and awareness of the organization's specific data resources and practices. By working across roles and maintaining their own growth, stewards foster a culture in which data literacy is developed, shared, and continually strengthened.

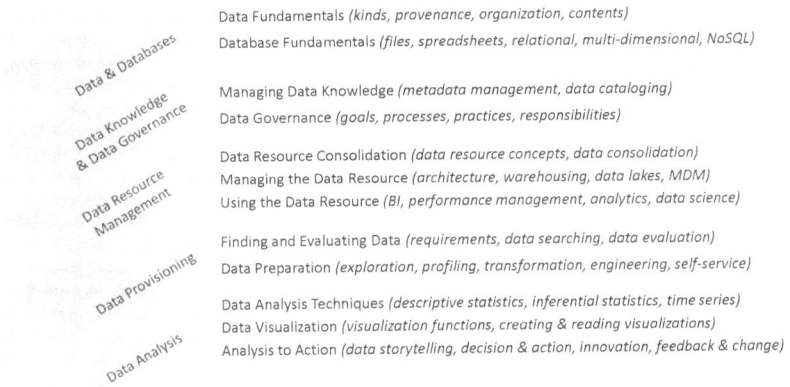

Data Fundamentals *(kinds, provenance, organization, contents)*
Database Fundamentals *(files, spreadsheets, relational, multi-dimensional, NoSQL)*

Data & Databases

Managing Data Knowledge *(metadata management, data cataloging)*
Data Governance *(goals, processes, practices, responsibilities)*

Data Knowledge & Data Governance

Data Resource Consolidation *(data resource concepts, data consolidation)*
Managing the Data Resource *(architecture, warehousing, data lakes, MDM)*
Using the Data Resource *(BI, performance management, analytics, data science)*

Data Resource Management

Finding and Evaluating Data *(requirements, data searching, data evaluation)*
Data Preparation *(exploration, profiling, transformation, engineering, self-service)*

Data Provisioning

Data Analysis Techniques *(descriptive statistics, inferential statistics, time series)*
Data Visualization *(visualization functions, creating & reading visualizations)*
Analysis to Action *(data storytelling, decision & action, innovation, feedback & change)*

Data Analysis

Figure 19: Essential knowledge areas for data literacy. See the full Body of Knowledge at eLearningCurve (tinyurl.com/ELC-DLBOK).

Cultivating Organizational Data Literacy extends these efforts to the enterprise level. Stewards promote a culture where questioning data is encouraged, definitions are shared, and tools are available to support learning. They connect assets such as glossaries, catalogs, and policies with daily work, making shifting literacy from abstract to practical. They advocate for literacy programs that build awareness across functions, encourage collaboration between business and technical teams, and reduce misunderstandings caused by inconsistent interpretation. Organizational literacy builds on individual capabilities. It is strengthened and sustained when data awareness is embedded into policies and workflows in ways that responsible use of data becomes part of normal practice, not an exception.

9.3 Data Ethics

Principles of Data Ethics guide how organizations handle data in ways that are fair, transparent, and respectful of individuals and society. Ethics is distinct from regulatory and legal compliance: regulations and laws establish what must be done, while ethics guide what should be done. Ethical principles often go beyond compliance requirements, setting responsible conduct expectations that go beyond compliance requirements. For stewards, this means working with principles such as privacy, ownership, transparency, and accountability, and helping others recognize that ethical choices are about more than simply following the rules.

	Quality	Privacy	Security	Compliance
Professionalism	What code of conduct exists? How should data ethics change it?			
Abuse	What is appropriate use? What are the risks of inappropriate use?			
Policy Gaps	Is existing policy inadequate, incomplete, or obsolete?			
New Policies	Do data ethics challenges create need for new data governance policies?			
New Issues	What ethical questions arise from data collection & data use activities and processes?			
Governance	How (and how quickly) must data governance and enterprise evolve?			

Figure 20: Data Ethics Management is a Multi-Dimensional Challenge.

Ethical Risks and Challenges often arise in ambiguous situations where there may be no single "right" answer. Trade-offs must be made between competing priorities, such as balancing business goals with customer privacy, organizational efficiency with fairness, or innovation with responsible use. Risks include biased data, misuse of personal information, and lack of transparency in algorithms. Stewards contribute by questioning assumptions, documenting limitations, and shaping discussions about risks and trade-offs that are explicit and inclusive of diverse perspectives.

Stewardship for Data Ethics is both advocacy and practice. Stewards help embed ethical principles into policies, metadata, and workflows, so ethical choices are intentional and supported—not left to chance. Stewards promote awareness of practical principles such as informed consent, confidentiality, and transparency, and they encourage teams to consider how data use affects stakeholders inside and outside the organization. By visibly acting with integrity, raising questions when trade-offs appear, and championing responsible behavior, stewards shape organizational culture and character, and they strengthen trust in data practices.

9.4 Data Orientation and Adoption

Data-Oriented Business Culture positions data as an integral part of strategy, decision making, management, and operations. It reflects a shared recognition that data creates value opportunities in many ways: guiding executive choices, informing management decisions, and enabling knowledge workers in their day-to-day work. A data-oriented culture expects decisions to be evidence-based, performance to be measured with reliable information, and business processes to be managed with awareness of the data they produce and consume.

Adoption of Data Practices involves embedding the responsible use of data into everyday work. Adoption is visible when people routinely turn to data for answers, apply governance standards, use shared definitions, create data with care, classify and document it properly, and share it in ways that promote reuse and trust. Stewards foster adoption by removing barriers to access, simplifying resources like glossaries and catalogs, and encouraging consistent practices for creating, using, and sharing data across teams and departments.

Barriers to Orientation and Adoption can limit progress even when resources are in place. Common challenges include a lack of trust in data, resistance to governance processes, unclear ownership, and limited data literacy. Organizational silos and territorialism also create obstacles, as do systems that are difficult to access and interpret. Stewards need to recognize these barriers because addressing them often requires cultural influence, cross-functional collaboration, and persistent advocacy.

Stewardship for Orientation and Adoption centers on advocacy and influence. Stewards model the behaviors they want to see, such as questioning the quality of data before acting on it and making definitions explicit in discussions. They also build trust by helping colleagues succeed in their use of data, making it easier to adopt new practices and integrate them into daily routines. In this way, stewards help create a culture where reliance on data is both natural and expected.

9.5 Data Value

Seeing Value is the foundation of data culture. It means recognizing data as much more than a by-product of operations. Value realization depends on seeing data as a source of insight, efficiency, and opportunity. When people see the value of data, they are likely to engage with it thoughtfully and use it to guide actions. Stewards help to shape data culture by drawing connections between data and real-world outcomes, highlighting where data has informed decisions, improved processes, and revealed new possibilities. Through examples and conversations, they encourage others to view data as a meaningful asset—not just something technical, but a valuable resource that helps to achieve goals and solve problems.

Preserving Value depends on mindsets, behaviors, and norms that prevent data decay as a result of neglect, misuse, and poor communication—factors that can quietly erode its usefulness over time. Inaccurate data, vague definitions, and loss of context reduce trust and make data difficult to apply effectively. Stewards help to shape data culture by exhibiting thoughtful data practices, calling attention to risks, and reinforcing the importance of clarity and care in data work. Through everyday actions, such as clarifying meaning, maintaining documentation, and making quality issues visible, they show that preserving data's utility is a shared responsibility. In doing so, they encourage a mindset where protecting the long-term value of data becomes part of how the organization works.

Creating Value is the cultural expression of curiosity, innovation, and purposeful data use. It involves more than having access to data—it requires people to ask new questions, combine information in creative ways, and apply data to improve outcomes. Stewards help to shape data culture by encouraging experimentation, supporting collaboration across functions, and helping others to work confidently with data. By simplifying access, clarifying context, and promoting the reuse of trusted data assets, they show how data can be a tool for insight and impact. In doing so, they foster a culture where creating value from data is routine and expected.

TEN

Master and Reference Data Management

Master and Reference Data Management focus on the types of data that provide shared context and consistency across business functions and systems. Master data consists of the core entities a business interacts with, such as customers, products, suppliers, and employees. Reference data is made up of codes and classifications that give categorical structure and meaning to business data, such as postal codes, product categories, and industry standard coding. While master data is created and updated within the organization, reference data is most often defined externally and adopted for internal use. Together, they form the backbone of data consistency across operations and analytics. For stewards, knowledge of how master and reference data are defined, maintained, and governed, including the processes that support them, is essential to ensure that these important data types remain accurate, consistent, and meaningful wherever they are used.

10.1 Master Data Management Basics

Master Data refers to the core entities that a business interacts with, such as customers, products, suppliers, employees, and locations. Unlike transactional data, which records day-to-day events, master data provides the consistent identifiers and attributes that give context to those transactions across systems. When well-managed, master data enables organizations to link activities, gain insight across functions, and operate with efficiency and accuracy.

Master data management (MDM) is the discipline that establishes processes, technologies, and governance to keep master data consistent, accurate, and aligned across the enterprise. Because master data is created and updated across multiple business functions, systems, and processes, maintaining alignment is an ongoing challenge. MDM addresses the problems that arise when different business functions, business units, and business systems maintain their own versions of the same entities. This leads to duplication, conflicts, and gaps in understanding. MDM's purpose is to maintain a consistent and reliable view of master data that supports both operational needs and analytical use.

Stewardship for MDM supports efforts to create and maintain a consistent view of master data entities across functions, systems, and processes. Stewards help assure that definitions are clear, standards are applied consistently, and quality checks are in place. They validate attributes, document rules, and provide coordination across teams to prevent changes from introducing conflicts and ambiguity. Stewardship reinforces the integrity of master data and its ability to provide shared meaning and value across the organization.

10.2 Master Data Management Processes

Core MDM Processes bring consistency and reliability to master data across systems. Parsing and standardization break data into usable parts and apply consistent formats. Matching and consolidation identify records that represent the same entity, resolve conflicts, and reduce duplication. Deduplication refines records by eliminating redundancies. Golden record creation provides a trusted single view of each entity. Together, these processes establish clarity and uniformity for the core data entities that span across multiple functions and systems.

Stewardship for MDM Processes helps to preserve business meaning and data quality as the technical work of parsing, matching, and consolidation is performed. Stewards validate definitions, confirm rules, and review quality thresholds so golden records reflect agreed standards. They help reconcile data inconsistencies, document assumptions, and advocate for consistency in how master data is understood. Stewardship involvement supports MDM processes, results that are technically consistent, and that business processes can rely on.

10.3 Reference Data Management Basics

Reference Data consists of the codes, classifications, and categories that give structure and meaning to other data. Examples include postal codes, country codes, product categories, and industry classifications. Unlike master data, which is created and updated within the business, most reference data is defined externally and adopted for internal use. Reference data is often small in volume but broad in influence, since it appears in many systems and supports consistency across transactions, reports, and analytics. When managed well, it supports terms and codes that are used and interpreted consistently throughout the organization.

Stewardship for Reference Data Management focuses on keeping this information current, accurate, and unambiguous. Stewards help prevent "drift," where codes and categories take on different meanings in different systems, and they work to align reference values across functions and platforms. They also ensure that changes to reference data, such as adopting a new standard or retiring an outdated code, are documented, communicated, and reviewed for impact. By guiding the management of reference data, stewards help maintain a shared language that supports both operational efficiency and reliable analysis.

10.4 Reference Data Management Processes

Managing Reference Data supports codes, classifications, and categories that are consistent, current, and aligned across systems. Processes include validating external sources, adopting standards, and updating values when external authorities change definitions. They also involve harmonizing reference data across multiple platforms so that codes and categories mean the same thing wherever they appear. Effective management of these processes prevents drift, duplication, and inconsistency in how reference data is applied.

Stewardship for RDM Processes supports the management of codes, classifications, and categories by reviewing changes for accuracy and clarity, documenting updates, and understanding impacts on downstream systems and reports. Stewards often facilitate communication about updates, making sure that business and technical stakeholders apply new codes and categories correctly. They also advocate for alignment between internal practices and external standards. By engaging in reference data management processes, stewards help ensure that reference data provides the reliable structure needed to connect and interpret other kinds of data.

ELEVEN

Information Management Concepts

Information Management Concepts provide data stewards with the background knowledge needed to understand how other roles work with and manage data. These roles include data architects, data engineers, systems engineers, database administrators, data creators, data consumers, data integrators, and many others. For stewards, the value of this knowledge is in seeing data management through the eyes of other stakeholders, which helps them bridge business and technical perspectives, place stewardship responsibilities in context, and connect business meaning with technical practices. This includes familiarity with architectural approaches such as data warehouses, lakes, fabrics, and meshes, as well as enough understanding of data models to interpret them and contribute business meaning to their development. Information concepts knowledge helps stewards to engage productively with both business and technical teams, support informed decision-making, and align stewardship practices with the ways data is managed and used throughout the organization.

11.1 Types of Data and Information

Structured, Semi-Structured, and Unstructured Data describe the different forms that data can take. Structured data is organized into rows and columns, making it easy to query and manage in relational databases. Semi-structured data, such as JSON and XML, has some organizational markers but does not fit neatly into tables. Unstructured data includes text, images, video, and other formats that require specialized tools to interpret. Understanding these categories helps stewards recognize the diversity of data they support and appreciate that stewardship practices must adapt to different data types and technologies.

Master, Reference, and Transactional Data represent different classes of data that serve distinct purposes in business operations. Master data describes core business entities, such as customers, products, and employees. Reference data provides standardized codes and classifications, such as country codes or product categories. Transactional data records the day-to-day activities of the business, such as sales, shipments, and service calls. By understanding these distinctions, stewards can better frame discussions about scope, quality requirements, and stewardship responsibilities across data domains.

Metadata as Information About Data is often described as "data about data." It provides the definitions, lineage, and descriptive context that make other data understandable and usable. Examples include business glossaries, technical descriptions, classifications, and data lineage records. For stewards, metadata is both a responsibility and a tool: they contribute to its creation and maintenance, and they use it to interpret and manage data consistently. Recognizing metadata as information in its own right reinforces its value as a resource that supports quality, compliance, and informed decision-making.

Operational and Analytical Data serve different purposes in the enterprise and are managed in different ways. Operational data supports day-to-day business activities, capturing transactions and events in real time to enable efficient execution of processes. Analytical data is prepared and organized for reporting, business intelligence, and advanced use cases such as forecasting and machine learning. Stewards benefit from understanding this distinction because quality expectations, governance needs, and data usage may vary between operational and analytical contexts. Recognizing these differences helps stewards mediate conflicts and support consistent interpretation across both environments.

11.2 Types of Data Stores

Files and File Systems are the most basic form of data storage, organizing information into individual files that can be stored locally, on servers, and in the cloud. Common formats include spreadsheets, text documents, images, and logs. File systems provide flexibility and simplicity but often lack consistent structure, metadata, and controls. For stewards, file-based storage matters because files often exist outside carefully managed systems, where applying consistent definitions, preserving context, and maintaining reliable access is difficult. These gaps create risks for compliance, governance, and long-term trust in the data.

Databases and Data Warehouses are used to store and manage structured data. Relational databases organize information into tables organized as rows and columns, and optimized to support efficient transactions and queries. Data warehouses use relational databases to integrate and consolidate data from multiple sources. Warehouse data is organized for reporting and analysis, with emphasis on historical, consistent, and curated content. For stewards, understanding database and data warehouse concepts helps to clarify meaning, reinforce consistent use across business and technical teams, and connect data practices to stewardship responsibilities for quality, access, and trust. This knowledge also supports governance and compliance needs, because warehouses are often central to regulatory reporting, audit requirements, and oversight of data used in business-critical decisions.

Data Lakes and Lakehouses store large volumes of diverse data, often in raw or lightly processed form. Data lakes are highly flexible, accepting structured, semi-structured, and unstructured content. Lakehouses are platforms that combine the capabilities of data lakes and data warehouses. They store diverse data types in large volumes, like a data lake, while also offering the management, governance, integration, and analytical structures traditionally associated with a data warehouse. These platforms are increasingly important in analytical and AI/ML contexts. For data stewards, understanding lakes and lakehouses is important because these environments shape how data is collected, organized, governed, and made available for advanced use. Awareness helps them address quality, clarify meaning, and guide responsible access so that data stored in these platforms remains usable and trustworthy.

Data Products package data to be delivered, shared, understood, and used with consistency. A data product brings together data, descriptive metadata, governance metadata, and processing. Products are accessed through an interface, such as an API, that receives data requests and delivers results. Encapsulating data as products provides reusable units that can be applied across domains and use cases. For stewards, data products highlight the importance of metadata that makes products findable, understandable, and usable. They contribute by documenting definitions, clarifying governance rules, and supporting quality expectations so products are reliable and trustworthy.

11.3 Data Architecture and Design

Operational Data Architecture organizes how data is captured and structured, and how it flows within systems that support daily business processes. In practice, these environments are often fragmented, spanning ERP platforms, SaaS applications, and legacy systems that have grown over time rather than being designed as a whole. The lack of integration creates disparities that frequently surface as stewardship challenges. Understanding operational data architecture helps stewards see where core business activities generate and rely on data, and where stewardship practices such as definitions, quality monitoring, and ownership can be applied. Understanding operational data architecture positions stewards to work closely with business units—the creators and consumers of data—to raise awareness of where the data people use originates, and by highlighting how the data created in one process supports downstream needs. In this way, stewards help bridge gaps between creation and use, fostering shared accountability across the flow of data.

Analytical and Integrated Architectures support data use beyond day-to-day transactions, enabling reporting, business intelligence, and advanced analytics. These architectures include warehouses, lakes, and lakehouses, as well as broader concepts such as data fabric and data mesh. Each approach makes trade-offs between control, agility, and scalability, and few organizations rely on just one. The result is often a mix of overlapping concepts and platforms, which adds complexity for data management and data stewardship. Stewards need to understand where analytical data comes from, how it is transformed, and what stewardship responsibilities apply in each setting. This knowledge equips them to clarify definitions when data is aggregated or repurposed, to document lineage that explains how results are produced, to evaluate quality and limitations before data is applied, and to facilitate conversations between business users and technical teams so that analytical outputs remain meaningful and trusted.

Master and Reference Data Design assures that critical shared information that provides context for business events and transactions is defined and managed consistently across the enterprise. Master data management (MDM) provides a single, trusted view of key entities, while reference data management (RDM) standardizes codes and categories. Stewards play a central role in MDM/RDM by validating definitions, guiding consistent usage, and supporting governance processes that keep master and reference data accurate and reliable.

Data Modeling creates structured representations of data that describe entities, relationships, and rules. Conceptual, logical, and physical models provide progressively detailed views of data, guiding how it is implemented in systems. Stewards are not expected to build models but should be able to read and interpret them, validate that business meaning is accurately represented, and contribute their knowledge of definitions and rules. Participation in modeling processes allows stewards to bridge business perspectives with technical design, helping to design models that serve both needs effectively.

11.4 Types of Databases

Relational Databases store data in structured tables with rows and columns, using keys to define relationships between entities. They are the most widely used database model for operational systems, supporting reliable transactions and consistent queries through the use of SQL. For stewards, understanding relational databases is valuable because so much core business data is stored in them, and stewardship responsibilities for definitions, quality, and access often start here.

NoSQL and Graph Databases provide alternatives to relational models, designed for flexibility and scale. NoSQL databases store semi-structured or unstructured content, making them suitable for high-volume web and IoT data. Graph databases represent data as nodes and relationships, enabling the discovery of connections, such as networks or fraud patterns. Stewards benefit from knowing these models exist, as stewardship practices such as metadata, lineage, and quality expectations must extend into environments that do not conform to traditional table structures.

Cloud-Native Databases are built to run in cloud platforms, offering elasticity, scalability, and managed services. They support a range of models—relational, document, key-value, and graph—while shifting responsibilities for infrastructure and performance to the provider. Stewards should understand that while cloud-native databases simplify operations, they also introduce considerations for data governance, protection, and compliance that stewardship helps to address.

11.5 Common Uses of Data

Operational Uses of Data focus on supporting the day-to-day activities of the business. Transactional systems capture sales, payments, inventory movements, and service interactions, while workflow systems support tasks such as logistics, scheduling, and customer service. Increasingly, IoT and automation systems generate operational data for uses such as manufacturing control, preventive maintenance, and real-time monitoring. Operational analytics is another key use, where data is applied directly within operations to improve processes—for example, route optimization in logistics or fraud detection in payments. Stewards need to understand these uses because quality and definition issues in operational data can have immediate and tangible business impacts. Equally important, stewards work directly with the business people who rely on operational data. Knowing who uses which data, and why and how it is used, helps to align definitions, resolve inconsistencies and conflicts, coach data consumers, and prioritize and resolve data management issues.

Analytical Uses of Data center on reporting, business intelligence, forecasting, and advanced analytics. Analytical environments consolidate and transform data to provide insights that guide strategy, optimize processes, and support innovation.

Modern analytical uses extend into machine learning and AI, where data is used to train models, generate predictions, and increasingly to enable agentic approaches that act on insights autonomously. Analytical results may be presented in dashboards, visualizations, or embedded into decision-support tools. For stewards, these uses are important because data is often redefined, aggregated, or repurposed differently from its operational sources, and stewardship supports interpretations that remain consistent, transparent, and trusted across various use cases.

Regulatory and Compliance Uses of Data involve meeting external obligations, such as financial reporting, industry regulations, and privacy requirements. Compliance uses demand that data be accurate, complete, and demonstrably trustworthy, with clear lineage and controls. Stewards support these uses by assuring that definitions are clear, policies are followed, and documentation is available to demonstrate compliance. They also act as connectors between business, technical, and compliance teams, helping to translate requirements into data practices and reinforcing the ongoing discipline needed to sustain compliance as regulations and business conditions change.

11.6 Business Data Flow

Data Creation and Capture happen whenever business processes generate new information—such as transactions, service requests, sensor readings, and customer interactions. Every process that creates data also serves other processes that depend on it, making awareness of downstream use critical. Stewards help business teams recognize the importance of the data they capture, clarify who relies on it, and reinforce practices that focus on accuracy and completeness at the point of creation.

Data Movement and Transformation carry data from the processes that create it to the processes that consume it, often through integration, enrichment, or aggregation. Data movement goes beyond technical to also represent handoffs between business functions, where misunderstandings or inconsistencies can create friction. Stewards play a role in facilitating collaboration between data creators and data consumers, and setting expectations for meaning, quality, and timing that are aligned as data flows across process boundaries.

Data Consumption and Feedback occur when data is applied to decision-making, reporting, analytics, or operational activities. Each use of data provides an opportunity to identify gaps, errors, or improvements that should be communicated back to the creators and maintainers. Stewards help establish these feedback loops, encouraging open communication between producers and consumers so that data quality, definitions, and processes improve over time. By framing consumption as part of an ongoing dialogue, stewardship shapes data flows that strengthen both business processes and organizational collaboration.

TWELVE

Data Stewardship and AI/ML

Data Stewardship and AI/ML is an emergent topic that raises questions, concerns, and uncertainties about the ways artificial intelligence and machine learning expand both the opportunities and the challenges of working with data. AI and ML are powerful tools, but they are highly dependent on the quality, consistency, and completeness of the data used to train and operate the AI models. Poor data in these contexts can lead to inefficiency, biased outcomes, unfair decisions, loss of trust, and very real social, economic, and legal consequences. For stewards, AI/ML introduces new areas of responsibility: affirming that data used in models is well-defined and traceable, advocating for ethical and responsible use, and staying alert to emerging regulations and standards.

Hot topics such as explainability, transparency, and ethics highlight the intensity of these challenges. While some argue that data stewardship will evolve to include AI stewardship, most experts expect AI governance and stewardship to emerge as distinct disciplines because the required responsibilities, skills, and knowledge are different. Recognizing this boundary helps prevent the steward role from expanding to an unmanageable scope while still emphasizing the importance of stewardship in building the strong data foundations on which AI/ML depends.

12.1 What is AI/ML?

Basic Concepts of AI and ML need to be understood to grasp how these technologies attempt to mimic aspects of human intelligence and learning. Artificial intelligence broadly refers to systems that can perform tasks requiring reasoning, pattern recognition, or decision-making. Machine learning is a subset of AI that builds models by training on data, identifying patterns, and making predictions or classifications. More recent advances include generative AI and agentic AI. Generative AI creates new content such as text, images, or code based on patterns and predictions. Agentic AI goes further by enabling systems to take actions, pursue goals, and interact with environments in ways that simulate autonomy. In practice, AI/ML shows up in many forms—from recommendation engines and fraud detection systems to generative and agentic tools now being adopted across industries. While the technical implementation may be complex, stewards need only a basic understanding of what AI and ML are, how they are used, and why they rely heavily on data. This understanding helps stewards support the quality, context, and ethical use of data in AI/ML initiatives, communicate effectively with technical teams, and guide business stakeholders in recognizing both the potential and the limitations of AI-driven results.

Dependence on Data is at the core of AI/ML. Models may be trained on historical data, real-time data, or both. The quality of that data strongly affects the accuracy, fairness, and trustworthiness of the results. If training data is incomplete, biased, or poorly documented, models may misrepresent reality or amplify harmful patterns. Because data defines both the capabilities and limitations of AI/ML, stewards play a crucial role in confirming that the data supporting models is well-documented, traceable, and aligned with agreed-upon definitions. Understanding this dependency helps stewards recognize why their contributions, such as clarifying definitions, documenting lineage, and raising concerns about bias, are critical to the responsible use of AI/ML.

12.2 AI/ML and Data Quality

Quality Dimensions for AI/ML Data apply directly to the performance and trustworthiness of models. Correctness tests confirm that data reflects reality accurately. Integrity preserves relationships and structure across datasets. Usability focuses on accessibility, clarity, and relevance of data to the model's purpose.

Objectivity—emphasizing absence of bias in collection, labeling, and representation—has become especially critical with the rise of AI/ML. Failures in any of these areas can lead to models that misclassify, exclude key perspectives, or embed systemic bias. For AI/ML, these risks are magnified, since errors in training data can scale across thousands of predictions and decisions.

Stewardship for AI/ML Quality emphasizes proactive involvement in shaping how data is prepared and maintained for model use. Stewards contribute by clarifying definitions, documenting lineage, validating assumptions, and raising questions about representativeness. They advocate for transparency in quality metrics, requiring thresholds and checks that are meaningful to business stakeholders and to technical teams. In addition, stewards highlight ethical concerns, emphasizing that objectivity and fairness are quality requirements that should not be compromised. Data steward participation in AI/ML initiatives helps to reduce risks of flawed data undermining model performance, accuracy, and reliability.

Monitoring Data Over Time is a distinct quality challenge for AI/ML. Models trained on a snapshot of data may degrade as patterns, populations, or behaviors shift—a phenomenon known as data drift. Stewards play a crucial role in defining what should be monitored, assuring that lineage and metadata capture data changes accurately, and advocating for model retraining and adjustments when the underlying data no longer accurately represents the current reality. Steward involvement helps keep

AI/ML systems relevant, reliable, and aligned with both business needs and ethical expectations.

12.3 Ethics and Responsible AI

Ethical Risks in AI/ML arise because models make decisions or recommendations that affect people's lives, often in ways that are not visible to those affected. Bias in training data can lead to discriminatory outcomes. Opaque models make it difficult to understand why decisions are made. Ethical risks extend beyond technical flaws, touching on fairness, accountability, and the potential for misuse. These concerns are sharper in AI/ML than in most other data contexts because of the scale and speed with which models act.

Explainability and Transparency are key responses to these risks. Explainable AI (XAI) focuses on making models interpretable, so humans can understand how inputs relate to outputs, why and how decisions are made, and why and how actions are taken. Transparency extends further, encompassing the disclosure of assumptions, data sources, limitations, and decision boundaries. Together, they help build trust by reducing the "black box" characteristics of AI. For data stewards, this means assuring that data lineage, metadata, and quality rules are readily available to inform explanations, and advocating for practices that make AI use transparent to stakeholders and to technical teams.

Ethical Use of Data in AI/ML is a central concern because collecting biometric, behavioral, and personal information without consent raises questions of privacy, autonomy, and fairness. Data ethics in this context extends beyond how models are built to include how data is acquired, labeled, stored, and shared. Stewards contribute by advocating for transparency in collection practices, promoting informed consent, and supporting alignment of data use with established ethical principles. The ethical dimension of data is directly tied to organizational data culture and reinforces the expectation that data is treated as a shared asset with responsibilities to those it represents.

Stewardship and Ethical AI involve more than documentation. Stewards act as advocates for fairness and accountability, raising questions about bias, challenging ambiguous practices, and reinforcing policies that govern the collection, labeling, and use of data. They also help connect ethical concerns to practical governance by making sure issues of objectivity and bias are treated as integral characteristics and requirements of data quality. By engaging with explainability, transparency, and fairness, stewards help organizations strike a balance between innovation and responsibility.

12.4 Governance and Stewardship Boundaries

Relationships of Data Governance and AI Governance are a subject of growing debate. Data governance provides structure and accountability for how data is defined, managed, and used. AI governance extends to include oversight of models, algorithms, outcomes, and the ethical use of data that feeds them. The two domains intersect because AI systems rely on data, but they are not the same. Governing a dataset and governing a model raise different challenges. For example, assessing lineage and quality in data differs from evaluating explainability, fairness, or accountability in an AI model. Recognizing this distinction is important so organizations do not assume traditional data governance is sufficient to manage the risks of AI.

Evolving Roles of Stewards reflect this distinction. Some suggest that data stewardship should expand into AI stewardship, but most experts believe AI stewardship will become a separate discipline because governing and stewarding models are radically different from governing and stewarding data. Still, stewards have a critical role at the intersection: they affirm that data used in AI/ML is well-defined, documented, and trusted, and that it is used responsibly in model training and operation. They also raise ethical concerns, transparency expectations, and compliance awareness in AI discussions, even if the responsibility for AI model governance lies elsewhere. Keeping a clear boundary prevents the steward role from becoming unmanageable and recognizes that AI stewardship requires different skills and knowledge from data stewardship.

12.5 Regulations and Standards

Evolving Regulatory Landscape is one of the biggest uncertainties for AI/ML today. Governments and standards bodies are only beginning to define frameworks for responsible use. Regulations in areas such as privacy (e.g., the GDPR), data protection, and consumer rights already indirectly affect AI, but new AI-specific rules are emerging, including the EU AI Act and early discussions in the U.S. and other regions. These frameworks address risk classification, transparency requirements, and accountability structures. As they are still developing, organizations face challenges in anticipating compliance obligations, and data stewards must remain vigilant to changes that could impact how data is collected, documented, and utilized in AI/ML.

Stewardship and Standards Alignment involves connecting evolving requirements to everyday data practices. Stewards help ensure that metadata, lineage, and consent records are documented in ways that support compliance audits. They advocate for practices that anticipate transparency and traceability requirements, even before regulations mandate them. They also play a role in monitoring alignment with emerging standards for ethical data use and fairness. By embedding stewardship into compliance and standardization efforts, organizations reduce risk and position themselves to adapt as AI/ML regulations mature.

Glossary of Data Management

Abstract Data Layer: A logical layer that provides standardized access to heterogeneous data sources by abstracting underlying complexity. See also: Data Abstraction; Data Virtualization.

Abstraction Layer: A conceptual layer that hides underlying technical complexity, enabling users to interact with data through simplified models. See also: Data Access Layer.

Access Control: The process of defining and enforcing permissions to read, write, or manage data. See also: Authentication; Authorization.

Accuracy: The degree to which data values correctly reflect the real-world objects or events they represent. See also: Data Quality Dimension.

ACID: A set of properties (Atomicity, Consistency, Isolation, Durability) that guarantee reliable transaction processing in relational databases.

Active Metadata: Metadata that is continuously collected, updated, and applied to automate and optimize data management processes. See also: Metadata; Data Observability.

Agentic AI: AI systems capable of autonomous goal pursuit, reasoning, and action-taking, often orchestrating multiple tools or processes without continuous human intervention. See also: Generative AI; Artificial Intelligence; Causal Models.

Aggregation: The process of combining multiple data records into a summarized form for reporting or analysis. See also: Data Summarization; Roll-up.

Agile Data Governance: An approach to data governance that emphasizes adaptability, iterative improvement, and responsiveness to business needs. See also: Data Governance.

Artificial Intelligence (AI): The use of algorithms and models to enable machines to perform tasks requiring human-like cognition, such as learning and reasoning. See also: Machine Learning; Deep Learning.

Anonymization: The transformation of personal data so individuals can no longer be identified, directly or indirectly. See also: De-identification; Data Masking.

Application Programming Interface (API): A defined method for applications or systems to communicate and exchange data. See also: Data Integration; Microservices.

Archival Data: Data stored long-term for legal, historical, or compliance purposes but not actively used in operations. See also: Data Retention Policy.

Artificial Neural Network (ANN): A computing model inspired by biological neural networks, used in machine learning for pattern recognition. See also: Deep Learning.

Atomicity: A property of ACID transactions that ensures each transaction is all-or-nothing, meaning all operations succeed or none are applied. See also: ACID; RDBMS.

Attribute: A property or characteristic of an entity in a data model. See also: Entity; Data Element.

Audit Trail: A chronological record of data-related activities, showing who accessed or changed data and when. See also: Data Lineage; Provenance.

Authentication: The process of verifying the identity of a user or system before granting access to data or systems. See also: Authorization; Access Control.

Authorization: The process of granting access rights to data, systems, or resources based on authenticated identity and assigned roles. See also: Authentication; Access Control.

Availability: A data quality dimension referring to the degree to which data can be accessed and used when needed. See also: Timeliness; Accessibility.

Baseline Data: The initial set of data used as a reference point for measurement or comparison.

Batch Processing: A method of processing large volumes of data at scheduled times, as opposed to real-time. See also: Stream Processing; Micro-batching.

Believability: A dimension of data quality reflecting the degree to which data is considered credible and trustworthy. See also: Data Quality.

Benchmarking: Measuring data management practices or quality against external standards or industry norms.

Business Intelligence (BI): Technologies, processes, and tools used to analyze data and present actionable insights. See also: Reporting; Analytics.

Big Data: Extremely large or complex datasets requiring specialized storage and processing technologies. Often described by the '3Vs': Volume, Velocity, and Variety. See also: Data Lake; Data Warehouse; Data Fabric; Volume, Velocity, Variety (3Vs).

Blockchain: A distributed ledger technology used to store, verify, and track transactions or records. See also: Smart Contracts; Distributed Ledger.

Business Data Steward: A steward responsible for guiding data definitions, quality, and uses that align with business needs. See also: Data Stewardship.

Business Glossary: A catalog of agreed-upon business terms and definitions to promote consistency across the enterprise. See also: Metadata; Data Catalog.

Business Metadata: Metadata that describes business meaning, rules, and usage of data elements. See also: Technical Metadata.

Business Process Modeling (BPM): The practice of representing business processes using standardized notations and diagrams. See also: Workflow Automation.

Canonical Data Model: A standardized data model designed to act as a common format for integration between systems. See also: Data Integration.

Cardinality: The number of elements in a set or the relationships between entities in a data model. See also: Data Modeling.

Categorical Data: Data values that fall into predefined categories, such as product type or gender.

Change Data Capture (CDC): A technique for identifying and capturing changes in data to propagate updates across systems. See also: Data Replication.

Chief Data Officer (CDO): An executive responsible for data strategy, governance, and maximizing value from data assets.

Cloud Data Governance: Governance practices adapted for cloud-based storage, processing, and analytics environments. See also: Data Governance.

Cloud Data Warehouse: A data warehouse built and operated in a cloud environment. See also: Snowflake; BigQuery; Redshift.

Cluster Analysis: A statistical technique used to group data points into clusters with similar characteristics. See also: Data Mining; Segmentation.

Completeness: The degree to which required data is present in a dataset. See also: Data Quality Dimension.

Confidentiality: A principle of information security focused on preventing unauthorized access to data. See also: Data Privacy.

Conformed Dimension: A dimension in a data warehouse that is shared across multiple fact tables for consistency. See also: Star Schema; Dimensional Modeling.

Consistency: A property of ACID transactions that guarantees a transaction brings the database from one valid state to another, enforcing integrity rules. See also: ACID; RDBMS.

Controlled Vocabulary: A standardized list of terms used to ensure consistency in labeling and classification.

Critical Data Element (CDE): A data element identified as vital for business operations, compliance, or reporting. See also: Master Data; Reference Data.

CRUD: An acronym for Create, Read, Update, Delete — the four basic functions of persistent storage.

Customer Master: A master dataset containing standardized and governed information about customers. See also: Master Data; Golden Record.

Data Abstraction: The process of simplifying data structures and hiding complexity to enable easier use and interoperability. See also: Abstract Data Layer; Data Virtualization.

Data Access Layer: A software layer that mediates between applications and data sources, standardizing access methods. See also: Abstraction Layer.

Data Architecture: The overall design and organization of data environments, including structures, processing pipelines, and architectural styles (such as data warehouse, data lake, data fabric, and data mesh) that support storage, integration, transformation, governance, and use of data.

Data Bias: Systematic distortion in data collection, processing, or interpretation that skews results or decision-making. See also: Data Objectivity.

Data Catalog: A centralized inventory that describes available datasets and their associated metadata to improve discoverability and usage. See also: Business Glossary; Metadata.

Data Classification: The process of categorizing data based on sensitivity, criticality, or usage. See also: Data Security; Confidentiality.

Data Custodian: An individual or group responsible for the safe custody, transport, and storage of data. See also: Data Owner; Data Steward.

Data Dictionary: A collection of descriptions of data elements, including meanings, formats, and allowable values. See also: Metadata.

Data Fabric: An architectural approach that provides a unified view of data across hybrid and multi-cloud environments. See also: Data Mesh; Data Virtualization.

Data Federation: A method of integrating data from multiple sources without physically moving it, using virtual queries. See also: Data Virtualization.

Data Governance: The exercise of authority, control, and shared decision-making over the management of data assets. See also: Data Stewardship; Governance Policy.

Data Integration: The process of combining data from different sources to provide a unified view. See also: Data Interoperability; ETL.

Data Interoperability: The ability of different systems and organizations to exchange and use data seamlessly. See also: Data Integration; Semantic Mapping.

Data Lake: A data storage architecture that holds raw, semi-structured, and transformed data in centralized repositories. Modern data lakes often include zones that separate raw, cleansed, and curated data, enabling both exploratory and governed use. See also: Data Lake Zones; Medallion Architecture.

Data Lake Zones: Logical layers within a data lake that organize data by refinement stage. Common zones include raw (bronze), cleansed (silver), and curated (gold), reflecting the medallion architecture approach to structuring data for progressive quality and usability. See also: Data Lake; Medallion Architecture.

Data Lakehouse: An architecture that combines features of data lakes and data warehouses to support both analytics and governance.

Data Lineage: The record of the origin, movement, and transformations applied to data as it flows through systems and processes. See also: Provenance; Audit Trail.

Data Manipulation Language (DML): A subset of SQL used to query and modify data. See also: DDL.

Data Mart: A subject-oriented subset of a data warehouse, typically organized for a business area, business process, business function, or workgroup, to support focused analysis and reporting. See also: Data Warehouse; OLAP.

Data Masking: The process of obscuring sensitive data values while maintaining usability for testing or analytics. See also: Anonymization; Pseudonymization.

Data Mesh: A decentralized data architecture that treats data as a product and assigns ownership to domain teams. See also: Data Fabric.

Data Migration: The process of transferring data between storage systems, formats, or applications.

Data Modeling: The practice of defining and analyzing data requirements, structures, and relationships. See also: Entity-Relationship Model; Dimensional Data Model; Semantic Data Model; Star Schema.

Data Monetization: The practice of generating measurable economic value from available data assets.

Data Objectivity: The degree to which data is free from bias, reflecting neutrality and fairness. See also: Data Bias.

Data Owner: The individual or group accountable for a dataset's use, quality, and compliance. See also: Data Steward; Data Custodian.

Data Pipeline: A sequence of data processing steps, often automated, to move and transform data from source to destination.

Data Privacy: The rights and processes that govern how personal or sensitive data is collected, stored, shared, and used. See also: Data Protection; PII.

Data Protection: The set of safeguards and legal measures to ensure the confidentiality, integrity, and availability of data. See also: GDPR; HIPAA.

Data Provenance: The documented history of data, including its source and changes over time. See also: Data Lineage; Audit Trail.

Data Quality: The measure of data's fitness to serve its purpose, typically across dimensions such as accuracy, completeness, consistency, and timeliness. See also: Data Quality Framework.

Data Replication: The process of copying data from one system to another to maintain consistency. See also: CDC; Synchronization.

Data Steward: A role responsible for overseeing data quality, definitions, and usage within a domain, including practices for adherence to policies and standards. See also: Data Owner; Stewardship.

Data Stewardship: The set of responsibilities and practices applied to manage data as a valuable resource. See also: Data Governance; Data Quality.

Data Strategy: An enterprise-wide approach to managing, governing, and leveraging data to achieve business goals.

Data Virtualization: A data integration technique that provides a unified view of data across systems without moving it physically. See also: Data Federation.

Data Warehouse: A centralized repository designed to support reporting and analysis by consolidating data from multiple sources. See also: Data Lake; OLAP.

Database: An organized collection of data managed by a database management system (DBMS). Databases may be relational, NoSQL, graph, document-oriented, or multimodal, storing structured, semi-structured, or unstructured data. See also: RDBMS; NoSQL; Document Database.

Database Administrator (DBA): A professional responsible for installing, configuring, maintaining, and securing databases.

Database Management System (DBMS): Software used to define, create, manage, and query databases. See also: RDBMS; NoSQL.

Data Definition Language (DDL): A subset of SQL used to define and modify database structures. See also: DML.

Descriptive Analytics: The analysis of historical data to understand past performance and trends. See also: Diagnostic Analytics; Predictive Analytics; Prescriptive Analytics.

Diagnostic Analytics: The analysis of data to determine why something happened, often using drill-downs and root-cause analysis. See also: Descriptive Analytics; Predictive Analytics; Prescriptive Analytics.

Dimensional Data Model: A data model designed for analytics that organizes data into facts and dimensions. See also: Star Schema; Snowflake Schema; Data Modeling.

Dimensional Modeling: A data modeling technique optimized for analytical databases and data warehouses. See also: Star Schema; Snowflake Schema.

Distributed Ledger: A database that is consensually shared, replicated, and synchronized across multiple sites. See also: Blockchain.

Document Database: A type of NoSQL database that stores data as JSON or XML documents. See also: Key-Value Store.

Domain: A logical grouping of data elements or responsibilities within a data management or governance framework.

Durability: A property of ACID transactions that guarantees once a transaction is committed, it remains so even in the event of a system failure. See also: ACID; RDBMS.

Entity: An object of interest in a data model, such as a customer, product, or order. See also: Attribute.

Entity-Relationship Model (ER Model): A type of data model that describes entities, their attributes, and relationships. See also: Data Modeling.

ETL Pipeline: An automated sequence of ETL jobs that move and transform data from multiple sources into a target system.

Event-Driven Architecture: An architectural style where events trigger data flows and system interactions in near real time. See also: Streaming Data.

Exploratory Data Analysis (EDA): An approach to analyzing datasets to summarize their main characteristics, often using visualization. See also: Data Profiling.

eXtensible Business Reporting Language (XBRL): A standard for exchanging business information. See also: Financial Data.

eXtensible Markup Language (XML): A markup language that defines rules for encoding documents. See also: JSON; Semi-Structured Data.

Extract, Load, Transform (ELT): A variant of ETL where data is first loaded into the target system before transformation. See also: ETL.

Extract, Transform, Load (ETL): A process that extracts data from sources, transforms it into a usable format, and loads it into a target system. See also: ELT; Data Integration.

Fact Table: A central table in a star schema that contains quantitative metrics for analysis. See also: Dimension Table.

FAIR Principles: A framework for making data Findable, Accessible, Interoperable, and Reusable. See also: Data Interoperability.

Federated Identity: An arrangement where a user's identity is shared across multiple systems, allowing single sign-on. See also: Authentication.

First Normal Form (1NF): A relational design rule requiring that data be stored in atomic (indivisible) values with no repeating groups. See also: Second Normal Form (2NF); Third Normal Form (3NF).

Flat File: A simple file-based data structure without hierarchical or relational links, often used for data exchange. See also: CSV; TSV.

Foreign Key: A field in a relational table that links to the primary key of another table. See also: Relational Database; Cardinality.

Format Standardization: The process of aligning data values to consistent formats, such as date or currency formats. See also: Data Quality.

Full Outer Join: A SQL join that returns all rows from both tables, with NULLs where no match exists. See also: Inner Join; Left Join.

General Data Protection Regulation (GDPR): A European Union regulation governing data protection and privacy for individuals. See also: Data Privacy; Data Protection.

Generative AI: AI systems that create new content such as text, images, or code based on learned patterns from training data. See also: Artificial Intelligence; Machine Learning; Agentic AI.

Golden Record: The authoritative, single version of a master data entity. See also: Master Data; Customer Master.

Governance Policy: Formal guidelines that define rules, roles, and responsibilities for managing data. See also: Data Governance.

Granularity: The level of detail represented in a dataset. See also: Data Modeling; Level of Detail.

Graph Database: A type of database optimized to store and query relationships using nodes and edges. See also: Property Graph; RDF.

Health Insurance Portability and Accountability Act (HIPAA): A U.S. law that mandates standards for protecting sensitive health data. See also: PHI; Data Privacy.

Hierarchical Database: A legacy database model where data is organized into tree-like structures. See also: Network Database.

Hybrid Cloud: An IT architecture combining on-premises, private cloud, and public cloud services. See also: Cloud Data Warehouse.

Identity Management: Processes and technologies that manage digital identities and control user access. See also: Authentication; Authorization.

Immutability: A property of data that cannot be altered once created, ensuring integrity and auditability. See also: Blockchain.

Index: A database structure that improves the speed of data retrieval. See also: Relational Database.

Information Architecture: The structure and organization of information assets to support usability and findability. See also: Data Architecture.

Inner Join: A SQL join that returns rows with matching values in both tables. See also: Outer Join; Full Outer Join.

Internet of Things (IoT): A network of physical devices embedded with sensors and software that collect and exchange data. See also: Streaming Data.

Interoperability: The ability of different systems or organizations to work together by exchanging and using information. See also: Data Interoperability.

Isolation: A property of ACID transactions that ensures concurrent transactions do not interfere with each other, preserving correctness. See also: ACID; RDBMS.

Java Database Connectivity (JDBC): An API for connecting Java applications to relational databases. See also: ODBC.

JavaScript Object Notation (JSON): A lightweight data format commonly used for APIs and document databases. See also: XML; Document Database.

Job Scheduling: The automated execution of data processing tasks at specified times. See also: Workflow Automation.

Key Performance Indicator (KPI): A measurable value used to evaluate success in achieving objectives. See also: Metrics; Data Analytics.

Key-Value Store: A type of NoSQL database that stores data as key-value pairs. See also: Document Database; Columnar Database.

Knowledge Graph: A graph-based representation of entities and their relationships, often used for semantic interoperability. See also: Ontology; Graph Database.

Latency: The delay between data creation and its availability for use. See also: Real-Time Data; Stream Processing.

Left Join: A SQL join that returns all rows from the left table and matching rows from the right. See also: Right Join.

Lineage: See: Data Lineage.

Logical Data Model: A representation of data elements and their relationships, independent of physical implementation. See also: Physical Data Model.

Lookup Table: A table used to map or standardize values across systems. See also: Reference Data.

Machine Learning (ML): A subset of AI where algorithms learn from data to make predictions or decisions. See also: Artificial Intelligence.

MapReduce: A programming model for distributed data processing, originally popularized by Hadoop. See also: Big Data.

Medallion Architecture: A data architecture pattern that organizes data into layers—bronze (raw), silver (cleansed), and gold (curated) — to provide progressively higher quality and business-ready datasets. Commonly applied in data lake and lakehouse environments. See also: Data Lake Zones; Data Lakehouse.

Metadata Management: Processes and technologies to capture, store, and use metadata for governance and analytics. See also: Metadata.

Microservices: An architectural style where applications are built as independent, modular services. See also: API.

Multi-Tenancy: A cloud architecture concept where a single software instance securely serves multiple customers (tenants), isolating their data and configurations while sharing underlying infrastructure. See also: Cloud Computing; SaaS.

Multimodal Database: A database that supports multiple data models (graph, document, relational) within one engine.

Natural Language Processing (NLP): A field of AI focused on enabling machines to understand and interpret human language. See also: Machine Learning.

Network Database: A database model where records are linked by sets in a graph structure. See also: Hierarchical Database.

NLP: A field of AI focused on enabling machines to understand and interpret human language. See also: Machine Learning.

Normalization: The process of organizing data in relational databases to reduce redundancy. See also: Relational Database; 3NF.

NoSQL: A category of non-relational databases designed for scalability and flexibility. See also: Document Database; Key-Value Store.

Online Analytical Processing (OLAP): Systems designed for fast querying and analysis of multidimensional data. See also: Data Warehouse; Cube.

Online Transaction Processing (OLTP): Systems optimized for managing transactional data with high volumes of simple operations. See also: Relational Database.

Ontology: A formal representation of knowledge with concepts, categories, and relationships. See also: Knowledge Graph; Semantic Layer.

Open Data: Data made available to the public without restrictions. See also: Data Sharing.

Operational Data Store (ODS): A database designed to integrate and store current operational data for reporting. See also: Data Warehouse.

Outer Join: A SQL join that returns matching rows plus non-matching rows from one or both tables. See also: Inner Join.

Payment Card Industry Data Security Standard (PCI DSS): A set of standards to secure credit card data. See also: Data Security.

Personal Health Information (PHI): Health-related information that can identify an individual. See also: HIPAA; PII.

Personally Identifiable Information (PII): Data that can be used to identify an individual, such as name or ID number. See also: Data Privacy.

Predictive Analytics: The use of statistical and machine learning techniques to predict future outcomes. See also: Prescriptive Analytics.

Prescriptive Analytics: The use of optimization and simulation to recommend actions based on predicted outcomes. See also: Predictive Analytics.

Primary Key: A unique identifier for records in a relational table. See also: Foreign Key.

Property Graph: A graph model where nodes and edges can hold properties. See also: Graph Database.

Provenance: The documented history of data, including its source and transformations. See also: Data Lineage.

Python: A widely used programming language for data science, machine learning, and data engineering, valued for readability and a rich ecosystem of libraries. See also: R.

Query: A request for data retrieval or manipulation in a database. See also: SQL.

Query Optimization: Techniques used by databases to improve query performance. See also: Index; Execution Plan.

R (Programming Language): A language widely used for statistical computing and data visualization. See also: Python.

RBAC: A method of restricting access to data based on user roles. See also: Access Control.

Real-Time Data: Data that is available immediately after collection. See also: Streaming Data.

Reference Architecture: A template solution that provides best practices for designing systems. See also: Data Architecture.

Relational Database: A database that organizes data into tables with rows and columns. See also: SQL; RDBMS.

Relational Database Management System (RDBMS): A DBMS based on the relational model using SQL. See also: ACID; SQL.

Right Join: A SQL join that returns all rows from the right table and matching rows from the left. See also: Left Join.

Role-Based Access Control (RBAC): A method of restricting access to data based on user roles. See also: Access Control.

Schema: A structural definition of data elements and their organization. In relational databases, schemas define tables and relationships. In semi-structured formats such as XML or JSON, schemas define embedded rules for structure and validation. See also: Data Modeling.

Second Normal Form (2NF): A relational design rule requiring that non-key attributes are fully dependent on the entire primary key. See also: First Normal Form (1NF); Third Normal Form (3NF).

Semantic Data Model: A high-level data model that describes the meaning and context of data. See also: Knowledge Graph; Ontology; Data Modeling.

Semantic Layer: An abstraction that translates complex data into business-friendly terms. See also: Ontology; Knowledge Graph.

Semi-Structured Data: Data that does not conform to a rigid schema but has some organizational properties, like JSON and XML.

Snowflake Schema: A type of dimensional model with normalized dimensions. See also: Star Schema.

Software as a Service (SaaS): A software delivery model where applications are hosted in the cloud and accessed via subscription.

Star Schema: A dimensional model with a central fact table connected to denormalized dimension tables. See also: Dimensional Modeling.

Streaming Data: Data that is continuously generated and processed in motion. See also: Real-Time Data.

Structured Data: Data organized into fixed fields, typically in rows and columns, such as those in relational tables. Structured data is highly standardized and easily queried using SQL. See also: Semi-Structured Data; Unstructured Data.

Structured Query Language (SQL): A standard language for managing and querying relational databases. See also: DML; DDL.

Tabular Data: Data organized into rows and columns, typically in spreadsheets or databases.

Taxonomy: A structured classification system for organizing data. See also: Controlled Vocabulary.

Temporal Data: Data that represents changes over time. See also: Time Series.

Third Normal Form (3NF): A database normalization form to ensure no transitive dependencies. See also: Normalization.

Tokenization: The process of substituting sensitive data with non-sensitive tokens. See also: Data Masking.

Transactional Data: Data generated by business transactions, such as sales or payments. See also: OLTP.

Trusted Source: A dataset recognized as authoritative and reliable. See also: Golden Record.

Unique Key: A constraint in relational databases ensuring all values in a column are distinct. See also: Primary Key.

Unstructured Data: Data without a predefined model, such as documents, audio, or video. See also: Structured Data.

Usability: A data quality dimension referring to how easily data can be understood and applied. See also: Data Quality.

Validation: The process of confirming that data conforms to defined rules and formats. See also: Data Quality.

View: A virtual table in a database created by querying one or more tables. See also: SQL.

Visualization: The graphical representation of data to support understanding and analysis. See also: Dashboard; BI.

Volume, Velocity, Variety (3Vs): The three defining characteristics of big data: scale, speed, and diversity. See also: Big Data.

Warehouse Automation: The application of automation technologies to manage data warehouse operations. See also: Data Warehouse.

Web Scraping: The automated extraction of data from websites. See also: Data Collection.

Workflow Automation: The use of technology to streamline and manage data-related processes without manual intervention. See also: BPM.

Index

abstract data layer, 117, 121
abstraction layer, 117, 121
access control, 117, 119, 131, 132
accountability, 9, 12, 13, 16, 55,
    60, 61, 62, 63, 86, 113, 115,
    116
accuracy, 3, 19, 21, 34, 44, 47,
    84, 92, 95, 107, 111, 117, 124
ACID. See Atomicity, Consistency,
    Isolation, Durability
active listening, 24
agentic AI, 118, 127
aggregation, 118
Agile, 118
AI, 33, 63, 72, 74, 101, 106, 109,
    110, 111, 112, 113, 114, 115,
    116, 118, 127, 129, 130
AI governance, 110, 115
analysis, 45, 46, 72, 73, 95, 100,
    118, 123, 124, 125, 126, 130,
    134
analytics, 16, 33, 39, 63, 71, 76,
    78, 79, 91, 94, 102, 105, 107,
    119, 120, 122, 123, 125, 128,
    129, 131
ANN. See artificial neural network
anonymization, 118, 123
API, 73, 118, 128, 129
archival, 118
artificial neural network, 118
atomicity, 117, 118

Atomicity, Consistency, Isolation,
    Durability, 117
attribute, 118, 125
audio, 46, 133
audits, 32, 52, 116
authentication, 117, 119, 126, 127
authority, 16, 55, 56, 57, 59, 60,
    61, 62, 63, 70, 122
authorization, 117, 119, 127
availability, 119
baseline, 119
batch processing, 119
believability, 119
benchmarking, 119
BI. See business intelligence
big data, 119, 129, 134
blockchain, 119, 125, 127
BPM. See business process
    modeling
business, 9, 10, 11, 12, 13, 14, 15,
    16, 17, 19, 21, 23, 25, 27, 30,
    31, 33, 34, 35, 36, 39, 41, 43,
    45, 46, 47, 48, 49, 50, 51, 52,
    53, 55, 56, 58, 59, 61, 62, 63,
    66, 67, 70, 71, 73, 77, 79, 84,
    85, 87, 88, 91, 92, 94, 95, 98,
    99, 102, 103, 104, 105, 106,
    107, 112, 113, 118, 119, 120,
    121, 123, 124, 126, 129, 132,
    133
business analysts, 14

135

www.ingramcontent.com/pod-product-compliance
Lightning Source LLC
Chambersburg PA
CBHW071424210326
41597CB00020B/3641